Primary Arts Education

Primary Arts Education:
Contemporary Issues

Edited by

David Holt

 The Falmer Press

(A member of the Taylor & Francis Group)
London • Washington, D.C.

UK   Falmer Press, 1 Gunpowder Square, London, EC4A 3DE
USA   Falmer Press, Taylor & Francis Inc., 1900 Frost Road, Suite 101, Bristol, PA 19007

First published in 1997

A catalogue record for this book is available from the British Library

ISBN 0 7507 0595 7 paper

Library of Congress Cataloging-in-Publication Data are available on request

Jacket design by Caroline Archer

Typeset in 10/12 pt, Garamond by
Graphicraft Typesetters Ltd., Hong Kong.

Printed in Great Britain by Biddles Ltd., Guildford and King's Lynn on paper which has a specified pH value on final paper manufacture of not less than 7.5 and is therefore 'acid free'.

Contents

Contents

Editor's Introduction

In recent times, those of us whose working lives are caught up with the enterprise of primary education have had much to bear. A tidal wave of change, much of which has appeared to be politically, rather than educationally or practically motivated, has engulfed the profession. As a result, many of the certainties of belief and practice which have hitherto sustained primary education have been inundated, and in some cases undermined or even swept away. Currently, we are in a period of relative calm, as the education system moves through the moratorium on substantial curriculum change that followed the Dearing Review. However, there will probably be more to come. Politicians of all persuasions now have such a highly developed taste for interfering in matters educational, that it hardly seems likely they will be able to restrain themselves once the prohibition is lifted, particularly since one of its effects will undoubtedly have been to quicken their appetites for further reform.

Against this background of turbulence and change, the fortunes of the arts in the primary school appear somewhat mixed. For example, although the language arts identified by the 1982 Gulbenkian Report are all clearly provided for within the Statutory Orders for English, the constant and growing obsession with basic literacy skills is just a little worrying in terms of arts education. More than a few teachers I meet these days claim that they no longer have time to read stories to their children, and casual observation in schools certainly suggests increasing amounts of time being devoted to formal language skills work. All this must leave some room for doubt as to whether the more creative and poetic use of language that once characterized good primary schools will survive, or simply go down under a welter of comprehension exercises and spelling tests. This, of course, is not to suggest that such skills are unimportant, but it is to question whether education — and particularly arts education — can ever be characterized simply by the practising of skills, rather than by the intelligent and purposeful use of such abilities in responding to experience.

Elsewhere, drama and dance have both been forcibly absorbed into other subjects, and it remains to be seen whether such an arrangement can possibly work to their advantage — or even guarantee their survival, in any real sense — in the longer term. Only art and music may perhaps be said to have prospered, given that both are now identified as foundation subjects within the National Curriculum, and presumably enjoy an enhanced status as a result. However, even this comfortable assumption may be open to question, given that within many primary schools, the core subjects and their associated testing regimes seem to be exerting increasing pressure. Not long ago, some of my art students reported being enthusiastically welcomed into a school by teachers who declared themselves unable to teach the subject 'because of National Curriculum'. Similarly, a group of primary curriculum leaders with whom I was working recently appeared frankly incredulous to learn that the quality of art education in their schools was also open to inspection by OFSTED. Like their colleagues in the first example, these teachers seemed to have assumed that, in spite of — or perhaps because of — its presence within the foundation, the subject was not really that important after all.

However, all this may perhaps be just a little too negative. Whilst recent events in the field of primary education have undoubtedly been extremely challenging, this does not necessarily justify the adoption of a victim mentality by those who are concerned for the role of the arts in education. It is still possible to find quality arts work going on within the primary system, and in some subjects — art would be a good example, despite the incidents mentioned above — even to wonder whether the reforms might not have improved matters a little by spreading some aspects of good practice rather more widely. In any case, primary educators are by nature optimistic, and it would therefore be odd indeed if a group of individuals with a wider interest in this field were not able to see the National Curriculum as providing opportunities, as well as problems. Accordingly, the intention of this book is to review the current situation with regard to primary arts education, and to look for signs of hope, as well as indications of difficulty, in this area. The general approach makes no pretence of being comprehensive, but simply represents the efforts of a group of colleagues at the University of Plymouth's Rolle School of Education to engage with the task identified above from the point of view of their own specific teaching and research interests.

The scope of their concerns is wide; initially, Rod Mackenzie provides a context for succeeding chapters by offering a cultural perspective on the situation of primary teaching and the arts in the 1990s. Whilst the tale he tells is not always an encouraging one, he nevertheless remains hopeful that good professional sense and creative teaching may yet overcome the more pedestrian approaches to pedagogy so often advocated within the contemporary debate. Of course, the quality of children's use of language frequently lies at the very heart of such discussion, and the language arts are therefore represented in a number of ways. Mim Hutchings, for example, examines ways in which children's own experience and their personal, idiosyncratic use of language may be deployed in order to support learning in the activity of story telling, and also considers to what extent current statutory requirements contribute to this objective; John Gulliver looks at the relationship between children's drawings and their written work, and raises some interesting issues with regard to the ownership and meaning of pupils' ideas within the classroom; and Elizabeth Housego argues strongly for a more optimistic and demanding view of children's ability to respond to literature than that which is enshrined within current documentation.

As an essentially bureaucratic enterprise, the National Curriculum has inevitably thrown up substantial problems of curriculum organization and delivery for primary schools; accordingly, Stephen Howarth and Christine Burns' chapter considers the problems which surround the idea of curriculum leadership in art, and questions the extent to which the role, as currently conceived, is capable of achieving its purpose in terms of quality control. David Holt, on the other hand, looks at a specific aspect of curriculum delivery within the classroom, and argues that — despite the current fascination with specialist teaching — the generalist approach nevertheless offers powerful advantages when applied to the teaching of art in the primary school.

Within primary education, the arts have often been used as a medium for learning elsewhere in the curriculum, and in some senses, the next two chapters relate this traditional role to contemporary National Curriculum concerns for personal, moral and spiritual development. Thus, Mark Halstead considers the ways in which the arts might contribute to the education of the human spirit, and argues powerfully for their deployment as a means of satisfying the spiritual hunger apparent amongst many young people. Similarly, Valerie Clark looks at ways in which it might be possible for arts activities to be used as a medium for exploring issues of death, loss and bereavement with young children. In the year of Dunblane, and a number of other lesser, but no less shocking, school tragedies, her contribution is both poignant and timely.

Elsewhere, the National Curriculum's concern to advance understanding of information technology throughout the subjects is thoughtfully addressed by Will McBurnie, who argues for a more selective and discriminating use of such approaches in order to raise the overall quality of primary music teaching. Finally, those arts disciplines which have been absorbed into other subjects are nevertheless also represented; David Coslett offers a fundamentally optimistic view, in which he suggests that there is still an opportunity for the teaching of drama to survive and grow within this new dispensation, not least because of the opportunities which it offers for primary teachers and children to explore the worlds of language, thought and imagination together. Janvrin Moore presents a fascinating insight into the realities of contemporary primary dance teaching. Her 'voices from the classroom' are drawn from a number of case studies, and they provide indications of the ways in which some primary teachers are beginning to come to terms with their new responsibilities with regard to this aspect of the arts.

In conclusion, a word of qualification. Inevitably, the book's approach is somewhat partial, both in terms of overall breadth and balance, and in respect of the unequal treatment which is accorded to individual disciplines and specific issues. However, matters could hardly be otherwise in an offering of this kind. Quite apart from the particular interests of individual contributors, the arts are a necessarily complex and diverse area of activity; similarly, within the current educational situation, some matters inevitably appear more pressing than others, and this sense of urgency also has an unbalancing effect. Accordingly, a uniformity of approach is rendered the more difficult. Nevertheless, a number of significant issues around primary arts education are identified and discussed, and readers should find the analysis provided either directly relevant to their own concerns, or else easily transferrable to similar situations elsewhere in the primary arts curriculum. In an educational environment in which the arts in the primary school clearly remain under threat, cross fertilization of this sort is important if a healthy stock is to be maintained, and it is hoped that this book will contribute something to the continuation of such debate.

1 A Cultural Perspective on Creative Primary Teaching and the Arts in the 1990s

Rod Mackenzie

This chapter considers the wider political and cultural context affecting primary education and offers some general background on creative teaching and the arts in the 1990s. Woods (1995, pp. 1–2) defines creative teaching as being 'reflective' rather than 'routine' involving 'holistic perceptions' of children and the curriculum and as being concerned with 'the affective as well as the cognitive' (p. 2) and the 'whole child'. Woods also indicates that creative teachers tend to see knowledge as 'indivisible' and are deeply knowledgeable of 'subject matter, pedagogy and pupils'. They have 'adaptability and flexibility', show both 'flair' and 'discipline' and are skilled in avoiding polarized views and resolving the dilemmas of everyday practice (Pollard and Tann, 1992). In the 1960s early pioneering versions of creative teaching associated with project work and the processes of the integrated arts were officially endorsed by the Plowden Report (CACE, 1967). By the 1990s, however, much had changed with the 'Three Wise Men Report' (Alexander *et al.*, 1992) criticizing 'Plowdenism' and marking the fact that child-centred teaching had finally fallen from 'official grace' (Darling, 1994, p. 108). Creative teaching through the arts also lost its previous place in the renewed utilitarian climate in which attempts to strengthen instrumental and vocational rather than personal and liberal education aims were made. These changes are reviewed here in order to set creative teaching within a longer perspective after World War II and to relate the gradual politicization of primary education after Plowden to the wider general context of cultural change. Against the prevailing stereotypes, it is suggested that primary teachers in general responded to social and cultural change by becoming increasingly reflective rather than ideological, and that this professional development was post-modern rather than progressive. A brief case study of a project based in the arts is considered in this light, and creative teaching is connected to cultural reconstruction and a democratic future.

Creative Primary Education After the Second World War

Attempts to put change in primary education in perspective might recall Herbert Read's (1943) *Education Through Art* because it synthesized so many pioneering insights and offered a vision of progress after the war. Read (1961, p. 8) gave very wide definition to 'aesthetic education' which he held could be advanced through the integrated arts, and argued that 'in a democratic society the purpose of education should be to foster individual growth' within the 'social group' (p. 9). He drew on John Dewey in advocating schooling for a democratic society and the project approach for primary education (p. 237). He also drew on Martin Buber's ideas of the central place of creativity and communion in education sustained through the quality of relationships made possible by class rather than specialist teaching (p. 230). Sybil Marshall's (1963) influential *An Experiment in Education* gave a practioner account of project work in this spirit in a rural primary school during the war and after. The arts were used to initiate a wide process of personal and social development through which opportunities to teach other skills and subjects were also pursued eclectically and holistically 'so that like a symphony, it is only completely satisfactory as an entire whole' (p. 172). Marshall tells us that she was 'headteacher and all the staff combined' (p. 14) and that there were about thirty children on roll some of whom were evacuees from the bombed London dockyard areas, others of whom had found the rural 'stillness' 'a greater ordeal than German bombs, and had returned to Bethnal Green' (p. 13). The school house had 'neither gas nor electricity' nor running water and she was six months pregnant. Despite this the achievements of the children across the curriculum were high, far beyond basic expectations. Marshall (1970, p. xi) later warned however against 'carrying the methods too far'. Despite Plowden's endorsement of the 'one per cent' of schools that were 'leaders of educational advance' (CACE, 1967, para. 270), Marshall saw that misunderstandings and false polarizations would 'set back' (*ibid.*, p. xii) creative teaching and it was not long before this came about.

Plowden child-centredness was first subject to various criticisms in fact by academics and researchers (for example, Cox and Dyson, 1969; Rodgers, 1968; Peters, 1969; Sharp and Green, 1975; Bennett, 1976; Alexander, 1984; Edwards and Mercer, 1987). However this critique was in its turn overtaken by political allegations of progressivism under successive Labour and Conservative governments from the 1970s onwards. The subsequent political interventions of the 1980s and 1990s buried the earlier professional debates under both the legislation and the accompanying rhetoric. Kelly (1995, p. 166) identifies an attempt to 'erase' the language of Plowden, and to replace it with a populist discourse which mixed free market consumerism with the controls of the National Curriculum and testing in the 1980s. In the 1990s, however, policy failure led first to the Dearing Report (1993), and then to further problems associated with class sizes and standards. This left primary education, like many other aspects of life in the 1990s, subject to deep political and cultural uncertainty. Pollard *et al.* (1994) point out, therefore, that there is a need to 'take stock' (p. 2) of the situation if vision is to be renewed, and this is approached here by first considering the politics of primary education after Plowden and then relating this to the wider cultural context.

The Politicization of Primary Education and the Myth of Progressivism After Plowden

The allegations of progressivism that precipitated the politicization of primary education after Plowden masked underlying economic realities. The optimism of the 1960s in fact foundered in the oil crises of the 1970s. Plowden's vision was overtaken by economic recession and 'back to basics' in education was initiated by Labour Prime Minister Callaghan's Ruskin College speech in 1976. Alexander (1994) summarizes:

> Despite the gap between progressivism in its pure form and what was actually going on in the majority of England's primary schools, primary teachers as a profession had to endure a barrage of media and political misrepresentation as progressivism and therefore they themselves, became the scapegoat for the country's educational and economic ills. This started shortly after Plowden, with the publication of the Black Papers, reached a peak in 1974–6 with the William Tyndale affair, Bennett's apparent demonstration that traditional methods were more effective than progressive and Callaghan's 'Great Debate', and then resurfaced in response to the publication of the Leed's report in 1991 . . . Primary education had become politicized: and truth, as always, was the first casualty. (p. 28)

In truth there is little evidence of progressivism in primary schools in the research and reports after Plowden (Bennett, 1976; Bealing, 1972; Barker-Lunn, 1982 and 1984). Galton *et al.* (1980) found that the realities in the 1970s were quite the opposite since two thirds of primary curriculum time was spent on 'fairly traditional' basics and noted that 'language and mathematics (or number) have formed the staple of the curriculum from the days of payment of results (1862)' (p. 78). Simon (1981) therefore concluded that the progressive 'revolution' was a myth. Despite research findings however the myth of progressivism was recycled in the run up to the 1992 General Election, the 'Three Wise Men Report' was commissioned, and the Office for Standards in Education pursued the issue subsequently (Galton, 1995). However the 'Three Wise Men' themselves had recognized that:

> The commonly held belief that primary schools, after 1967, were swept by a tide of progressivism is untrue. HMI in 1978, for example, reported that only 5 per cent of classrooms exhibited wholeheartedly 'exploratory' characteristics and that didactic teaching was still practised in three-quarters of them. (Alexander *et al.*, 1992, para. 19)

Alexander (1995, p. 286) thus notes that it was only a minority who kept a 'network' of creative teaching alive in a discouraging climate. However there were further general professional developments in the late 1970s and 1980s.

7

Blenkin and Kelly (1981) identified a mixture of elementary, child-centred and developmental traditions influencing practice at this time, an analysis broadly echoed by others (Richards, 1982; Golby, 1986). Alexander (1988, p. 167) thus described 'competing imperatives' operating which Mackenzie (1983) found created a 'hybrid' approach. Nias (1989) noted the holistic 'craftmanship and artistry' (p. 197) involved in balancing multiple expectations which intensified with the advent of the National Curriculum. Pollard *et al.* (1994, pp. 12–14) also indicate that through the 1980s the 'strengthened professionalism' (p. 14) of teachers was evident and that this was associated with the growth of 'reflective teaching' (Pollard and Tann, 1992), which will be considered later in the chapter. Pollard *et al.*'s research into the effects of the incoming National Curriculum in the early 1990s found that 'about one fifth' (p. 101) of teachers at Key Stage 1 employed 'creative' (p. 99) strategic responses associated with reflective teaching. The need for reflection if the hybrid mixed condition of primary education is to be mediated and enacted remains clear, as is the need for wider reflection on the political and cultural context (Zeichner, 1995).

The 'back to basics' theme also developed further important social and cultural layers in the 1990s which had been lying dormant. Traditional cultural concerns on the Right led to pressure for National Curriculum subject rewrites from 1990 onwards. Ball (1994, p. 7) identified an increasingly 'authoritarian' and nationalistic curriculum emerging and warned that 'political' rather than 'economic' reasons underlay this development. This climate was initially fuelled by the Conservative General Election victory in 1992, and then by uncertainties created by economic recession, European Union and the ending of the Cold War. The murder of the pre-school child James Bulger in 1993, and the head-teacher Philip Lawrence in 1995 added further dimensions of moral panic. Kelly (1995, p. 151) identifies a preoccupation with 'law and order' developing in the mid 1990s, as education policy showed reemergent concerns with moral, social and cultural cohesion and control (NCC, 1993; OFSTED, 1994), which were pursued through initiatives from the Schools Curriculum and Assessment Authority (for example, Tate, 1996).

In summary it can be concluded that in reality primary teachers were more conservative than progressive in the 1960s and 1970s and that there is some evidence that they became increasingly reflective in the 1980s. A gap between political rhetoric and professional realities was thus opened and widened, and the wisdom of basing policy on the myth of progressivism and using teachers as scapegoats becomes questionable at a number of levels. First the hostile climate discouraged creativity and this meant that the improvements promised by reflective teaching had to develop in a climate of constant misrepresentations. Second the assumption that the centralized control of education could bring improvement was itself ill founded, as the subsequent problems of the National Curriculum and testing illustrated. In retrospect it is thus the accountability of politicians rather than that of primary teachers that comes into question. Also a third concern arises with the nationalization of the curriculum which initially had economic and vocational justifications but then acted as a Trojan horse for promoting 'traditional' cultural values. Campbell (1995) questions such 'over-weening ambition' in using 'the state apparatus for control of beliefs and values' (p. 2); Kelly (1995) also argues that democracy itself was threatened; and the dangers of losing local checks and balances on central ideology is noted by Simon and Chitty (1993). However, beyond the political a longer cultural perspective suggests that Plowden was a late expression of the forward looking hopes of progress after the war, which could be achieved broadly by encouraging creativity in teachers and children in their local schools. In the early 1990s, however, this vision and trust were quite lost and a pessimistic, nostalgic, backward looking outlook prevailed so that control rather than creativity became dominant. These changes can now be considered as reflections of the mixed cultural conditions of modernity and post-modernity developing from the 1960s to the 1990s.

Aspects of Modernity/Post-modernity and Post-modernism

First some definitions are needed. The term 'culture' itself has multiple meanings, here it is used in the wider sense developed by Williams (1976) as 'a whole way of life, material, intellectual and spiritual' (p. 116). Kearney (1988) offers initial definition of the field when he states that 'modernity is where we grew up' whilst 'post-modernity is where we now live' (p. 18). There is no clear break between the two conditions however, particularly in times prone to nostalgia, and so the conditions co-exist and are related rather than sequential (Smart, 1993).

Modernity is associated with the Enlightenment ideals of emancipation and progress and is connected with the belief that the world can be changed for the better through rational organization and science. Hartley (1994a) indicates that it requires:

> a Puritan temper, Weber's 'iron cage of bureaucratic rationality', a work ethic. Its production process is typified by mass production, clear demarcation of task, hierarchy and an interventionist state . . . There are grand theories to explain it . . . there is a 'central value system' into which we are said to be socialized, there is uniformity, certainty, a grand design. (p. 88)

Critics claim, however, that the ideals of modernity associated with human freedom are in practice prone to degeneration into technocratic controls (Usher and Edwards, 1994). The promises of progress, it is claimed, have faded throughout the century following world wars, the holocaust, the nuclear threat and economic and ecological problems (Hall *et al.*, 1992). Gradual human disillusion creates what Lyotard (1992) identifies as postmodern 'incredulity toward metanarratives' of legitimation (p. xxiv). Usher and Edwards (1994) explain:

> . . . in the condition of post-modernity there is a questioning of the
> modernist belief in a legitimate . . . centre upon which beliefs and
> actions can be grounded. Science and faith in an inevitable progress
> provided such a centre, an 'authorizing' position from which control
> could be exerted and sociocultural hierarchies legitimated through a
> process of 'mastery'. With the questioning of the legitimacy of mastery
> and the accomanying 'decentring' of knowledge, modernist certainty
> is undermined with consequent uncertainty pervading thought and
> action. Post-modernity, then, describes a world where people have to
> make their own way without fixed referents and traditional anchoring
> points. (p. 10)

Post-modernity is thus a *mood* or *attitude* engendered by disillusion with the
power and knowledge settlements of modernity to which however it is inextricably related. Smart (1993, p. 15) therefore claims that we are 'living in an
interregnum' between times, where as Gramsci (1971) put it 'the old is dying
and the new cannot get born'.

'Post-modernism' refers to a set of human responses to this cultural interregnum which have 'weak' and 'strong' expressions (Squires, 1993, p. 3). Kelly
(1995, p. 73) argues for a balanced position between modernist and post-
modernist extremes, avoiding the polarization of absolutist 'ultimate certainty'
or of relativist 'complete scepticism', and this is the position adopted here
(Smart, 1993). Kelly (1995) refers to the 'epistemological revolution' (p. 63) in
the twentieth century which brings a 'more tentative, less dogmatic view of
knowledge' (p. 62) in which people develop their own perspectives. 'Perspectivism' is thus an alternative to the absolutist/relativist opposition, and is characterized by a rejection of such polarizations on the grounds that in practice life
is more mixed and that some cooperation rather than automatic adversarialism
is required. Usher and Edwards (1994) relate perspectivist knowledge to the
'*practices* of everyday life' rather than to a 'transcendent and invarient set of
values' and claim that the acceptance of perspectivism does not 'court irration-
ality and paralysis' but foregrounds public 'dialogue, practical engagement and
a certain kind of self referentiality' (p. 27).

Three very broad overlapping post-modern options can be identified in
responding to the present cultural interregnum. These can be typified as attempts to restore the past, to live for the consumerist present or to reconstruct
the future.

Cultural Restorationism

O'Sullivan (1993) identifies a 'new fundamentalism' as a 'direct response to
what is taken to be the relativism of post-modernity' (p. 26). Hall (1991) defines this as the impulse '. . . to restore coherence, 'closure' and Tradition in the
face of hybridity and diversity' (p. 311). Restored certainty is thus attempted in

calls to go 'back to basics' and reproduce aspects of an imagined golden past (Smart, 1993).

Consumerist Culture

Alternatively, there are the consolations and seductions of consumerism and the new technologies (Featherstone, 1994). This is perhaps the most common image associated with post-modernity. Bauman (1992) however renews the long critique of the 'duplicities' of 'choice' and 'freedom' underlying consumerism and its effect on people and the planet (pp. 224–5).

Cultural Reconstructionism

Beyond these, however, a third 'reconstructive' possibility opens (Thompson, 1992). This is typifiable as a collective intellectual coming of age beyond the older ideological metanarratives. A cultural reconstructionist outlook might offer a positive vision of inclusive democratic citizenship and ecological concern (Giddens, 1994) and the diversity of 'post-colonial' identity and life style (McRobbie, 1994).

These cultural perspectives all carry curricular reflections and implications and can now be brought to bear on previous discussion of the growing politicization of primary education after Plowden in order subsequently to consider the effects on primary teachers in the 1990s.

Primary Education, the ERA and Modernity/Post-modernity

Hall (1991) brings cultural perspectives to bear on political developments in the 1980s when he describes Thatcherism as a project that attempted 'regressive modernization' (p. 118). Hall indicates that Thatcherism employed the powerful central controls of modernity to create a mixture of free market and 'Victorian values' in order to reverse postwar developments in society. This project, therefore, combined both the freedoms of cultural consumerism and the controls of cultural restorationism. Hartley (1994b) detects this powerful combination reflected in the 'mixed messages of education policy' of the time in which:

> the legitimatory rhetoric of ownership, choice and diversity accords with the consumerist culture of an emerging post-modernism. But the close specification of both educational targets and funding has all the hallmarks of the age of modernity. (p. 242)

Thus many of the problematics of modernity outlined previously can be identified in the introduction of the ERA. The forceful, interventionist, bureaucratic centralism coupled with the certainty and closure represented in the 'grand design' features of the legislation, all clearly reflected the characteristics of modernity. Kelly (1995) cites the nationalization of the curriculum, the absolutist view of knowledge as grammar school subjects, and the power-coercive manner of their imposition as key features of this. Regressive modernity was also evident in the 'industrial' and 'commercial' (p. 162) metaphors used to describe the 'delivery' of education packaged in the rhetoric of consumerist 'choice' and Craft (1995) describes this mixture as constituting the 'McDonaldization' of education (p. 125). It can be concluded, therefore, that Campbell's (1993) description of how the ideals of the National Curriculum as 'a dream at conception' turned into a technocratic 'nightmare at delivery' exactly reflects the long-standing troubles of modernity.

In the 1990s Ball (1994, p. 5) identifies the curriculum rewrites of the 1990s before Dearing, as being driven by 'neo-conservative cultural restorationism' creating 'curricular fundamentalism' (p. 39). Hartley (1994a) refers to a sense of cultural 'panic' due to the perception that:

> post-modernism is not a culture, is not a shared way of seeing the world, is not a unifying narrative. There are no canons anymore. But from this panic may come calls for 'basics', for fundamentals, for collective rituals and identities based on nationhood, race, gender, religion: in short, for some kind of return to the grand ideas of the age of modernity: for a return to certainty — for reestablishment of the disestablished. (p. 90)

Ross (1995a) comments:

> Contemporary social movement in Britain is not seen by the government as simply post-modernist phenomena, but as a breakdown of the old order and certainties, an unacceptable moral pluralism, a lack of identity associated with the loss of empire, the disintegration of the welfare state and relative economic decline. Faced with the collapse of what had formerly constituted the nation, the government is now part of a movement to invent a new nation in its place. (p. 98)

Hargreaves (1994, p. 5) points out that in post-modernity 'economic regeneration' is thus increasingly conjoined with 'national reconstruction' and attempts 'to resurrect traditional values and senses of moral certainty' and place new emphasis on 'cultural unity and identity' through education. Ball (1994) concludes that education thus became part of 'culture wars' aimed at the 'depluralization' (p. 7) of society. The question that arises at this point is where did this cultural conflict leave primary teachers professionally?

Primary Teachers as Post-modern Reflective Practioners and the ERA

Reflective teaching in the 1980s is considered first in order to go on to question the effects of legislation upon it in the 1990s. Hartley (1994b, p. 84) identifies the rise of the 'niche narratives' of the reflective practioner in the 1980s as being in keeping with the times and agrees with Wilkin (1993) that this was a 'post-modern development' (p. 35). Thus primary education in the 1980s might be seen in a new light, as reflecting complex contemporary cultural developments which were post-modern, rather than progressive (Kelly, 1995). Nias's research on primary teaching in the 1980s would seem to support this conclusion (Nias, 1989, pp. 197–201). The eclectic balanced pragmatic qualities identified by Nias — combining 'interpersonal', 'pedagogic' and 'coping skills' which teachers deployed in living with the dilemmas and uncertainties of practice — made up the 'artistry and craft' of post-modern reflective teaching. Alexander (1984, p. 152) too had defined the intellectual process of such 'everyday theorizing' as requiring 'independence coupled with receptiveness and adaptability', involving 'scepticism toward certainties' and understanding the 'tentativeness and paradox' involved in thought and knowledge (p. 173). Pollard and Tann (1992) also indicated the 'open-mindedness' required in reflective practice which suggested a typical post-modern suspicion of the fixed prescriptions of ideology. In this respect Golby (1988, p. 30) had identified the damage done by 'over-simple' ideological categories of an 'either-or' nature and had concluded that primary teachers had been more 'adept' than academics at avoiding such mistakes (Blyth 1988). Thus Pollard *et al.* (1994) suggest that the growth of reflective teaching in the 1980s led to 'the disposition to draw eclectically on a range of teaching approaches' (p. 14). These were 'underpinned by new understandings about children's learning and the active role of teachers' (*ibid.*) beyond the old damaging polarization of traditional teaching as telling and progressive learning as doing and the related opposition of utilitarian vocational aims and more personal and humanistic aims, which may now be briefly considered.

Advances made from the Piagetan structuralist base following the seminal work of Vygotsky (1962 and 1978) and Bruner (1986) stress the role of language and the social and cultural in learning. The Piagetan emphasis on the individual construction of meaning had thus been extended to a post-structural position now commonly referred to as *social contructivism* which stresses the social supports which scaffold learning given by adults, or by peers and thus deconstructs the older opposition of teaching and learning. Pollard (1996) offers diagrammatic representations of the earlier polarized behavourist and constructivist accounts of teaching and learning (see figures 1.1 and 1.2) contrasted with the more holistic social constructivist approach (see figure 1.3). Bruner (1986, p. 123) thus stresses that the perspectivism of the new position depends not so much on set 'canonical roles' as on a cultural 'forum' which 'must express stance and invite counter-stance and in the process

Rod Mackenzie

Figure 1.1: *A behaviourist or transmission model of a teaching and learning process*

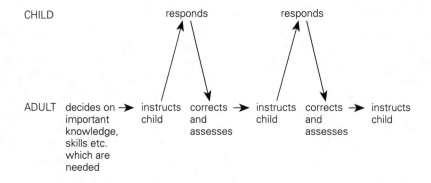

Figure 1.2: *A constructivist model of a teaching and learning process based on interpretations of Piaget's work*

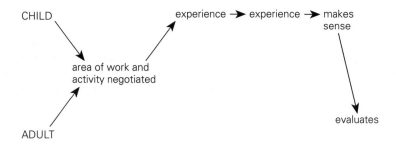

Figure 1.3: *A social constructivist model of a teaching and learning process based on the work of Vygotsky and Bruner*

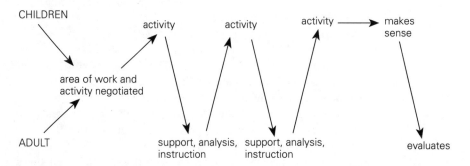

leave place for reflection, for metacognition' (p. 129). Edwards and Mercer (1987) also emphasize that this 'is a social process, not merely one of individual discovery but one of sharing, comparing, contrasting and arguing one's perspectives against those of others' (p. 164). Edwards and Mercer suggest that the work of Vygotsky and Bruner thus allows for 'a third step' beyond the false dichotomy of 'traditional' and 'progressive' ideology (*ibid.*, p. 36). Lather (1992) also indicates that in post-modern perspectivism 'binary either/or positions are being replaced by a both/and logic' (p. 90). Pollard *et al.* (1993) therefore speculates that the social constructivist position has 'the potential to offer a new legitimation' (p. 175) to primary practice, and this suggests further potential for a reconstruction of both curriculum and culture which will be explored later in the chapter.

First, however, the fate of reflective teaching following the introduction of the ERA must be considered. Opinion about the effects of state policy on teachers generally in the 1990s is divided. Smyth (1987) considers the international tendency to use technocratic controls on teachers, whilst Zeichner (1995) notes that some forms of reflective teaching are also vunerable to such control because they focus blindly on technical means to the ends set by others. Hill (1991) and Ball (1994) claim that the intention of the ERA was to turn teachers into state 'technicians' and agents of cultural restorationism, but intentions are not the same as outcomes and the effects of the legislation on the emerging professionalism of reflective primary teaching in the 1980s were more mixed. Alexander (1994) and Galton (1995) for example indicate that the advent of the National Curriculum and its subsequent rewrites did not sweep away the legacy of the primary hybrid. In the early 1990s Pollard *et al.* (1994) did not find, for example, that the elementary tradition had been restored to pride of place in the schools they studied. The evidence suggested that the National Curriculum and other initiatives intensified the complexity of the primary hybrid rather than resolving it in one direction or another (Woods, 1995). In fact the original legislative overload led to the teachers' boycott of testing in 1993, which gathered strength in alliances and created a domino effect on policy leading to Dearing. Whilst it is clear that Dearing did not resolve the original flawed assumptions of the ERA, the important recognition of the *principle* of professional disecretion did reemerge. Also, social alliances formed at that time continued to campaign on the issues of class sizes in the 1990s. Dearing may be taken, therefore, as marking a post-modern moment when professional and public force began to push the state back, or more simply as a device through which the Government side-stepped and lived on. However Dearing is construed, the fact that the Government was forced to admit the need for review was a demonstration that in post-modernity power was in professional and public as well as in political hands. Pollard *et al.*'s (1994) research thus indicated that teachers were not:

> puppets pulled by the strings of policy makers . . . as teachers attempt to reconcile external demands with their belief in professional autonomy

and with the practicalities of the working situation they must make choices about the way they carry out their work . . . they effectively become makers of policy and might be seen as 'practical policy makers' in their own classrooms. (p. 78)

Pollard *et al.* (1994) thus identified a variety of professional strategic responses to the National Curriculum in the early 1990s and concluded:

It seems to be the case that the exercise of coercive power has challenged some teachers to explore their professional repertoire in order to find ways in which they can mediate the new requirements or incorporate them into existing practices. (pp. 237–8)

We may now turn to one case of this drawn from the work of a creative teacher towards the end of the 1995 summer term which offers an example of the continuation of post-modern reflective teaching under the National Curriculum. The case study also illustrates aspects of the nature and possibilities of creative teaching in the 1990s.

Creative Teaching in the 1990s

The following consideration of aspects of some arts-based project work with a class of 10-year-olds draws on the teacher's and children's perspectives of the purpose of such work. The school is large and serves an urban area where there is high unemployment and where many contemporary urban problems are evident. The school had come through OFSTED inspection well six weeks before the work considered here. Within the large junior department three classes in year 5 had collaborated in work focused on a number of National Curriculum targets drawn from the Dearing curriculum. The classes had undertaken a project based on the Greek story of Theseus and the Minotaur which involved a strong emphasis on collaborative group work and the integrated arts with each class working towards a separate class play. In the class considered here the degree of the responsibility given to the children to research, write, direct, act and stage their own play marked it out. The richness of the work across the curriculum, the balanced style of teaching and learning and the degree of challenge for both the teacher and the children indicated the presence of creative teaching. The teacher explained:

I have been interested in this holistic way of working for a long time. In the seventies we called it 'integrated studies', in the eighties we called it 'real problem solving'. For me it has always been a logical way to make connections for the children between various areas of the curriculum to show how the jigsaw pieces fit together. Giving the children responsibility and more control of their learning, depending on how much different groups can handle, means that my role changes to planning and setting them off and then offering support and advice on demand, although I intervene if they get lost. I also help them to review how it's going with circle time and constant discussion, We talk all the time but the point is I don't *just* 'tell' them or leave them to 'discover', I try to get them to accept more and more responsibility, to lead them on, to negotiate and set targets, to be confident, to grow up, it's hard! I want them to develop 'poise', to develop the ability to plan personally and with a group, to respect themselves and the others *and* to be critical.

There are clear connections here with some of the features of post-modern reflective teaching discussed above. This teacher's professional participation in networks of creative teaching in the 1970s and in developments in the 1980s such as the National Oracy Project were of obvious importance. Her uses of the creative forms and processes of the arts were very much in evidence and were inseparable, it must be stressed, from her concern to develop other skills and subjects. The integrated arts were used also however as a means toward personal and social education and as a way of teaching the children how to learn, rather than simply as desirable activities or ends in themselves. In many ways, therefore, her work was in the long tradition of holistic creative teaching from Sybil Marshall onward, and it is timely to note its continuing existence and to take stock of its nature and purposes. This is approached here through considering some aspects of the review the teacher and the children made of the Theseus project in its last stages. The value of reviewing work in promoting independent learning through self and peer assessment is well recognized now (Fisher, 1995). The children in this class had operated review processes from their first term in the class when they had undertaken a maths and science project involving presentations of experiments with bridge building. Their teacher used a Socratic questioning approach to review inviting the children to tell her and each other about the process of the work and their own development (Chamberlin, 1989; Lipman, 1991). The brief extracts from these conversations used here are taken from one of the tapes made by the teacher, in this case with six children drawn from the other small groups the children had decided to form which divided responsibilities between script writing, direction, costumes, props and research.

At the outset of the project the teacher told the children the story of how Theseus found his way through the labyrinth to kill the Minotaur, building up rich archetypes of hero, journey and monster. In addition the childhood, youth and maturation of Theseus were highlighted with particular emphasis on overcoming challenges and the place of human relationships in this process. The children's own challenge of producing their play was thus deliberately set in a richly allusive context which encouraged the children to move beyond the literal to the metaphoric through the practical and imaginative work involved in building the play. The teacher guided the children through such connections, supporting them in linking their past and present experience to reflections on the future. In the review for example the children reported that being responsible for making their own play was a challenge to which they could not have risen had they not had previous experiences of group work, particularly in the bridges presentations. However, the children felt that it had been a major growth point for them, and recommended that it should be repeated with future classes. They saw themselves as having developed self and social confidence and reflected on the stages of their development. It should be understood that the 'joint understanding' Edwards and Mercer (1987, p. 1) found being constructed in primary teaching is not easy, by definition, to enter from the outside, particularly not when it takes the deeper form that it did here. However, common themes in the children's perceptions of the process they had been through did emerge clearly as they used the review process to look back to the bridges group work and tie the year together, and then to begin to look forward. This process and some of the emerging themes can be illustrated through the experience of two of the children whom I will call Emma and Tracey. Emma had struggled with writing and performing the narration and was 'devastated' when it had to be rewritten at one stage, although this had been mastered finally:

> *Emma*: Not to be boasting but when me and Mary first got to know the narration off by heart we felt really pleased and we wanted to tell everyone that we'd learnt it off by heart and we wanted to read it straight away to the whole class.

> *Tracey*: She really got on with it, like sometimes she doesn't get on with it, this time she really got on with it and she didn't mess around or anything. She just sat down and thought about it and then just wrote it.

Emma's success in playing her part in the group contrasted with earlier problems with the bridges group work in the first term which she looked back on now:

> *Emma*: I was with Lindsey, Daniel and Justin and they were getting really frustrated with me because I was just like telling them what to do and saying if you don't get on with this bridge I'm really going to go for you . . . When I was first in a group I couldn't work properly and now I've worked more in a group and I've learnt to cooperate and to stop being bossy. When we first did this play I thought: Oh no I'm never going to be able to do this in a group! But when I actually settled down in my group because there were people I actually liked to work with in that group, um I thought maybe I have got a chance of working.

Tracey: Emma's grown up a lot, like in assembly she used to muck around a lot. Now she can listen.

Emma: (hesitantly)   I wanted to be Tracey's friend for ever and the only way to do that was to show off.

Tracey: Yes.

Teacher: (gently)   And what have you decided about that now?

Emma: Well she likes me better the way that I actually am. . . .

Teacher: I think that's a terrific thing to say that you've managed to recognize that, you've faced your own Minotaur there really haven't you?

These exchanges illustrate something of the complex process of self and social reflection at work, and how the children made connections across time and different activities and used this to deepen their insight. The theme of 'growing up' stressed by Tracey underlies the whole exchange summarizing the self and social gains made and indicating the connections rather than the opposition between the two. What Edwards and Mercer (1987, p. 1) describe as the 'mutuality of perspectives' at work in such social group experiences allows individual reflection to emerge and the teacher is able to encourage Emma to a degree of metacognitive movement. At the same time the teacher works at the leading edge of the children's understanding, so that whilst celebrating Emma's achievement, she is able also to offer a metaphoric perspective, which will be considered further later. First though some further extracts elaborate the general theme of 'growing up'.

Tracey was in the group that had taken responsibility for directing the play, and she had found the coordinating role involved in being a director very challenging. The problem here was the opposite of Emma's tendency to over-assertiveness. Tracey reported that the directors had problems in:

Tracey: . . . organizing everybody because they don't listen to you they don't look up to you like they do to teachers.

Teacher: Has that improved? Have you got better?

Tracey: Yes it has because now we're not like embarrassed or any-thing to shout quiet or tell what to do not ask them what to do because at first, I don't know about them, but I was embarrassed because that they would laugh because you had to tell them what to do so I always asked them . . .

Tracey (and Emma together):   Can you do this, can you do this . . .

Teacher: So instead of saying 'can you' what did you end up doing?

Tracey (and Emma together):   Do this, Do this!

(General laughter)

Teacher: So you became more assertive . . .

Here the teacher leads the children further in and supplies a summarizing perspective for them. What was being worked and reworked in a complex spiralling process in the review as a whole, were shared understandings of what it is to exercise independent self and social control balanced, for example, beyond Emma's description of herself as having been too 'bossy' and Tracey's description of being too 'embarrassed'. All the children recognized how much they had grown since the bridges work in being open to other ideas and in learning from each other. John enjoyed being in the props group for example because 'everybody cooperates and like if there's something to do they'll do it' by 'locking onto group work to get ideas'. David agreed: 'We got our heads together'. This kind of growth process was in fact a common pattern of experience reported by the children:

Mary: You'll find it hard to co-operate, but once you've learnt to listen to other people's ideas its not so bad and you can face the class and tell them your ideas.

John: It'll help you to grow up because if you're silly the class won't take you seriously and the play won't happen.

Tracey: It's quite hard to control the class but if you try to control yourself and think about what you're going to say before you say it, it's easy.

The importance of cooperative learning of this kind is increasingly recognized (Fisher, 1995), and the growth of the 'poise' and maturity the teacher had wished to promote was clear. The teacher found that gains in learning how to learn through group process also connected with individual advances in other skills and subjects. She found that parents too were aware of the change in their children and their increased ability to direct both their own lives and school work. The children also made further connections with their future where they saw both assertiveness and cooperative team work as central to education and employment chances:

Kate: It could help you in the future if you wanted to have a career as a teacher or like a lecturer where you have to stand out in front of lots of crowds or classes or universities when you get there it can help you to speak out and not be shy . . .

David: . . . if you go to a big company there'll be loads of people round you all the time so you so you get used to loads of people and you won't be shy to work with someone, to listen to them and share.

Reflections on the future were also supported by the teacher's introduction of the term 'metaphor' at the beginning of the review. The following exchange brought the review to an end:

Kate: The labyrinth is like showing your life really going through stages . . . like when you're born it could be the start of the labyrinth, then when you go on is when you're grown up, and then when you get to the Minotaur that's when you die.

(General laughter and cries of Yes!)

Mary: . . . in the story it sounds like Theseus had an easy life before he learns what really happens, so it can be easy but it gets harder.

Teacher: So we have a challenge to face?

Emma: Yes it's like Mary said before when you go out in the labyrinth you go through it . . . it could also teach you to be careful life is a very precious thing and we must be careful with it.

Mary: Yes, life is precious so you can't muck around with it.

Kate: I feel like a snail because if you're really shy you want to keep inside you're own shell you don't really want to go outside or anything you just want to be you're own person, don't want to know anybody else, don't want to go out . . . (laughs) . . . you crawl along slowly.

Teacher: And once you've got rid of your shell what happens then?

Kate: You're free and you just like enjoy yourself.

Teacher: . . . You've just made a metaphor, do you understand what I mean by a metaphor? Go on then Jenny.

Jenny: It means making something into something else, and making it mean something different.

These brief extracts illustrate some gains emerging from the spiralling process of the review, which itself reflected the overall process of the Theseus project. The nuances and subtleties of such holistic educative processes are not easy to do justice to, but their power in supporting human growth in terms of both self and social assertion and integration and in promoting the general maturation of young people is evident. The use of common metacognitive and metaphoric processes to support a culture where the importance of both independence and interdependence are supported promises much at both school and societal levels. Creative teaching of the kind reviewed here suggests the holistic overcoming of the false oppositions between the individual/social, teaching/learning, cognitive/affective, personal/vocational and so forth which underpin the traditional/progressive polarization in education. Post-modern reflective practice of this kind thus offers some possibilities of a way forward beyond the educational conflicts that have obscured the vision of progess expressed after the war and which the cultural conflicts of the 1990s have deepened. The future of such creative teaching in relation to curriculum and cultural reconstruction can now be considered.

Creative Teaching and Curriculum and Cultural Reconstruction in the Future

In this chapter creative teaching through the arts from World War II to the 'culture wars' Ball (1994) identified in the 1990s has been considered. It has been argued that the politicization of primary education after Plowden was based first on a myth of progressivism and secondly increasingly employed regressive modernity to attempt curriculum and cultural restoration by constraining and controlling the creativity of teachers. However, in reality creative teachers of the kind endorsed by Plowden were few in number and it is questionable whether the term 'progressive' ever described their practice adequately. There was also a wider increase of professionalism in primary teachers in the 1980s despite the discouraging climate, but this was reflective rather than ideological, post-modern rather than progressive, holistic rather than partisan. An illustration of creative teaching through the integrated arts drawn from the period following the Dearing Review was next considered in order to illustrate both the continuation and the nature of a holistic approach in the 1990s. This work promoted the personal and social development of the children beyond the older polarizations that have obscured proper debate of purpose and pedagogy in primary education from Plowden onwards. The future of creative teaching in post-modernity in relation to professional, political and cultural perspectives may now be considered.

Professional debate in the mid-1990s is beginning to turn its attention to the future again, beyond the preoccupations with the politicization of the past period. Alexander (1995), for example, takes stock of the hybrid state of primary education following the ravages of failed policy leading to Dearing.

Alexander notes that the attempt to restore the elementary school utilitarian tradition appears not to have swept away other primary traditions, and asks how far a 'progressive model' (p. 310) might now be a useful 'counter-balance' to the utilitarian emphasis of the past period. Silcock (1993) also argues that 'misconceptions and misrepresentations' were involved in the critiques of progressivism and attempts to redress this by tracing the contours of a 'new progressivism' (p. 107). However, although it is good that such professional debate is reemerging from the wreckage of policy in the 1990s, it is doubtful whether it will be helpful to conduct the debate in the old ideological language. I believe that the recovery of a professional agenda from the politicization of the past period will not be assisted by this, since it can be seen that in many respects it has been this language which failed to describe the reality of practice that has been the problem. This is one reason why post-modern discourse has value because it avoids further fruitless polarizations, and supports both more critical and more creative approaches to describing and developing practice (Usher and Edwards, 1994). What is now required may be more difficult for those academics and politicians who are unable to go beyond the modernist habits of polarization, adversarialism and hierarchy, than for those primary teachers who have learnt the holistic arts of post-modern reflective practice. However since what is needed now is nothing less than an articulation of both the purpose and pedagogy of primary education fit for the future, everyone involved will be challenged. Pollard (1990) associates this quest with a 'new professionalism' (p. 75) based on reflective teaching, which now needs to be developed further. In addition Pollard *et al.* (1993) note the potential that social constructivism has for constructing a new 'legitimation' of primary practice beyond the old polarized conflicts, as suggested by the case study above (p. 175). In their research into the effects of the ERA on primary teachers Pollard *et al.* (1994) in fact found a 'significant minority' (p. 99) of teachers alive to the possibilities of a new professionalism based on 'creative' ways of working with both children and the National Curriculum. As was noted previously Pollard *et al.* found 'about one fifth' (p. 101) of their sample of teachers working in this way, but speculated on larger numbers adopting more creative approaches as the Dearing Review of the National Curriculum and testing settles.

Politically, however, Dearing's unfortunate continuation of the core/foundation divide perpetuated the old dichotomies of utilitarian vocational aims with more humanistic personal aims (Golby, 1994). The merely utilitarian will be strengthened further if inspection, testing and league tables emphasize the core subjects at the expense of other educational and cultural concerns. Further conflict and debate therefore seems likely, and policy will continue to run into real problems so long as it does not take into account the holistic insights that practice can offer in avoiding the problems of the past period. Such problems inevitably followed the political raising of consumerist expectations whilst scapegoating teachers in order to mask the continued underfunding of primary education as post-modernity advanced. However the accountability of teachers which had been the dominant theme from the 1970s onwards, was joined by the accountability of politicians in the 1990s as failed policy increasingly boomeranged on the Government, and both parents and the public became increasingly sceptical of the promises and probity of politicians. It would seem, therefore, that the advance of post-modernity in these respects will continue to beset the Government of any political colour until either expectations are lowered or promises are funded adequately (Mackenzie, 1995). Hartley (1994b, p. 243) indicates the risks for all involved when he speculates that 'Eventually diversity, voice and choice may prove to be postmodern conditions which the mandarins of modernity may find it hard to contain.' Whether the political attempt to scapegoat teachers for what is essentially an economic, political and cultural problem in resolving the size, scope and funding of the welfare state and the purposes of schooling will serve future governments as it has in the past is moot. The problem for politicians now is that both parents and the public have become more sophisticated and less gullible and are not so easily controlled or infantilized. This uneasy and unsure public coming of age in the 1990s is that aspect of post-modernity that was previously described as cultural reconstructionism to which we may now turn.

In the longer cultural perspective it can be seen that what has been lost since the war is a sense of vision. The hopes of progress in school and society from the middle of the century have given way to post-modern pessimism at its end. When faith in the future fails, cultural and curriculum restoration and the consolations of consumerism may seem to provide defences against cultural fear. However these defences were always contradictory since consumerism with its emphasis on the freedom of the market, eroded the very social and cultural fabric which the restorationists wished to conserve. In the 1990s it can be seen increasingly that cultural restorationism and many aspects of consumerism are forms of escapism and are flights from both the realities and the possibilities of cultural change. It is here that the real choices ahead emerge and the need to recover a sense of hope and possibility in both curriculum and cultural terms emerges (Aronowitz and Giroux, 1991). Beyond the retreats from reality that have been such powerful and prevalent constituents of post-modernity, there are other cultural and curriculum possibilities with which to face the future in a more measured way. At the cultural level the challenges ahead for both individuals and society arguably require creative rather than defensive responses. It is true, on the other hand, that the post-modern emphasis on choice and diversity will need to be reconciled with a degree of unity, and a new balance of forces will need to be established (Squires, 1993). However these tensions are not new and can be understood as part of what Williams (1983) typified as a 'long revolution' in moving towards more democratic societies, which Carr (1995) and Kelly (1995) indicate now needs to be renewed. In other words it is democracy itself that provides the unity in diversity needed, rather than some attempted restoration of the central control of thought, belief and values (Giddens, 1994). Human diversity and difference is considerably older than post-modernity and the path to democratic citizenship has always been accompanied by fears that increased democracy must bring disorder and chaos. Beyond such fears, however, a renewed vision reconstructing both culture and curriculum might recognize that cultural diversity within a democratic framework is part of a creative solution to the times rather than the problem that restorationists fear it to be. This cultural perspective therefore carries implications for curriculum reconstruction in which education for democracy assumes a new overall prominence. Again, such proposals have precedents, since Dewey (1916) broached this earlier in the century it has been abundantly evident that the development of a democratic society needs democratic schooling (Kelly, 1995; Chamberlin, 1989). Richards (1982) in fact identified such a position in relation to the primary curriculum as being focused on 'social democracy' (p. 12) and Alexander (1988) noted that this implied concern that the curriculum should:

> enable the child both to fulfil individual potential and to contribute to societal progress. The latter defined in terms of plurality, democracy and social justice, as well as the economy. (p. 157)

Updating and developing such democratic aspirations, however, for both curriculum and culture carries implications for the school, the family and the workplace (Mouffe, 1993), as well as more generally for the political and cultural institutions of a 'learning society' (Ranson, 1994). It is in this context, that the potential of holistic creative teaching of the kind considered in the case study can be understood because of its capacity to induct young people into the processes of a democratic way of life (Siraj-Blatchford, 1995). The children's perspectives on their personal and social growth and its relevance to their future suggests some aspects of the rich potential (Ross, 1995b). The purposes of primary education pursuing these democratic ends can be summarized generally as being to develop communicative and culturally competent citizens (Gilbert, 1995), and the integrated arts would clearly have a central role to play in promoting this. In cultural perspective it can be seen that in the 1940s pioneers like Herbert Read and Sybil Marshall developed creative teaching within the context of World War II when democracy, as a political system, was at risk. In the cultural confusions of the 1990s arguably once again the challenge is to develop and to extend democracy as the quality of a whole way of life, rather than to restrict it to a simpler concern with equality of the vote, important though this remains (Laclau, 1993). It is here that an understanding is needed that creative education could produce creative citizens able to develop beyond the problematic interregnum of post-modernity, in terms of both quality and equality. Such an understanding begins to suggest a renewed vision of primary education for democracy and to indicate the urgent need for the further development of such perspectives in both policy and practice.

In conclusion it is clear that primary teachers in the mid-1990s, no less than other members of society, are faced with the cultural uncertainty of post-modernity and that this has posed professional problems which need resolution.

Woods (1995) concludes that there is an unresolved struggle in primary education in the mid 1990s and that teachers are caught 'betwixt and between' (p. 8) worlds, and that this reflects the general cultural conditions. Pollard *et al.* (1994) note the 'stark' value clash between the 'new market ideology' of the 1980s and early 1990s emphasizing 'competition and consumerism' and the more person centred values of many primary teachers (p. 232). Beyond this clash, however, the absolute opposition of personal and vocational aims for primary education is in many ways false, if longstanding throughout the century (Silver, 1983). It has been argued here that holistic and creative teaching offers a way forward beyond such habitual oppositions and could play a part in renewing a democratic future based on inclusive citizenship. But this requires the professional not to lose sight of both personal and social dimensions in creating a relevant education for children focused on their rights and responsibilities both as children and as future democratic citizens. Pollard (1990) had argued earlier that the incoming legislation would require teachers to have 'the self-confidence to stand up for what they believe in, and to develop actively into the future' (p. 75). It has been suggested in this chapter that a creative approach to primary education in which the arts will be central has much to offer in creating a curriculum fit for such a cultural future. This approach has been associated with a new professionalism based on postmodern reflective teaching increasingly informed by a social constructivist pedagogy and it has been suggested that it would be given a sense of direction by a cultural reconstructionist purpose appropriate to the further development of a democratic society.

References

ALEXANDER, R. (1984) *Primary Teaching*, London, Cassell.
ALEXANDER, R. (1988) 'Garden or jungle? Teacher development and informal primary education' in BLYTH, W.A.L. (Ed) *Informal Primary Education: Essays and Studies*, London, Falmer Press.
ALEXANDER, R. (1992) *Policy and Practice in Primary Education*, London, Routledge.
ALEXANDER, R. (1994) *Innocence and Experience: Reconstructing Primary Education*, APSE Paper No. 5, Stoke, Trentham Books.
ALEXANDER, R. (1995) *Versions of Primary Education*, London, Routledge.
ALEXANDER, R., ROSE, J. and WOODHEAD, C. (1992) *Curriculum, Organization and Classroom Practice in Primary Schools: A Discussion Paper*, London, HMSO.
ARONOWITZ, S. and GIROUX, H. (1991) *Postmodern Education: Politics, Culture and Social Criticism*, Minneapolis MN, University of Minnesota.
BALL, S.J. (1994) *Education Reform: A Critical and Post-structural Approach*, Buckingham, Open University Press.
BARKER-LUNN, J. (1982) 'Junior schools and their organizational policies', *Educational Research*, **24**, 4.
BARKER-LUNN, J. (1984) 'Junior schoolteachers and their organizational policies', *Educational Research*, **26**, 3.

BAUMAN, Z. (1992) *Intimations of Postmodernity*, London, Routledge.

BEALING, D. (1972) 'The organisation of junior school classrooms', *Educational Research*, **14**, 3.

BECK, C. (1990) *Better Schools — A Values Perspective*, London, Falmer Press.

BENNETT, N. (1976) *Teaching Styles and Pupil Progress*, London, Open Books.

BENNETT, N. and DUNNE, E. (1992) *Managing Classroom Groups*, Hemel Hempstead, Simon & Schuster.

BLENKIN, G.M. and KELLY, A.V. (1981) *The Primary Curriculum*, London, Harper and Row.

BLYTH, W.A.L. (Ed) (1988) *Informal Primary Education: Essays and Studies*, London, Falmer Press.

BRUNER, J. (1986) *Actual Minds, Possible Worlds*, London, Harvard University Press.

CACE (1967) *Children and Their Primary Schools*, Vol. 1., London, HMSO.

CAMPBELL, J. (1993) 'A dream at conception: A nightmare at delivery' in CAMPBELL, J. (Ed) *Breadth and Balance in the Primary Curriculum*, London, Falmer Press.

CAMPBELL, J. (1995) *Education 3–13*, **23**, 2.

CAPRA, F. (1982) *The Turning Point — Science, Society & the Rising Culture*, London, Wildwood House.

CARR, W. (1995) *For Education: Towards Critical Educational Inquiry*, Buckingham, Open University Press.

CHAMBERLIN, R. (1989) *Free Children and Democratic Schools*, London, Falmer Press.

COX, C.B. and DYSON, A.E. (Eds) (1969) *Fight For Education: A Black Paper*, London, Critical Quarterly Society.

CRAFT, A. (1995) 'Cross-curricular integration and the construction of the self in the primary Curriculum' in AHIER, J. and ROSS, A. (Eds) (1995) *The Social Subjects Within the Curriculum: Children's Social Learning in the National Curriculum*, London, Falmer Press.

DARLING, J. (1994) *Child-Centred Education And Its Critics*, London, Chapman.

DEARING, R. (1993) *The National Curriculum and its Assessment: Final Report*, London, School Curriculum and Assessment Authority.

DES (1978) *Primary Education in England: A Survey by HMI*, London, HMSO.

DEWEY, J. (1916) *Democracy and Education*, New York, Macmillan.

EDWARDS, D. and MERCER, N. (1987) *Common Knowledge*, London, Methuen.

FEATHERSTONE, M. (1994) *Consumer Culture & Postmodernism*, London, Sage.

FISHER, R. (1995) *Teaching Children to Learn*, Cheltenham, Stanley Thornes.

GALTON, M. (1995) *Crisis in the Primary Classroom*, London, Fulton.

GALTON, M., SIMON, B. and CROLL, P. (1980) *Inside the Primary Classroom*, London, Routlege & Kegan Paul.

GAMBLE, A. (1983) 'Thatcherism and conservative politics' in HALL, S. and JACQUES, M. (Eds) *The Politics of Thatcherism*, London, Lawrence and Wishart.

GIDDENS, A. (1994) *Beyond Left and Right*, Oxford, Polity Press.

GILBERT, R. (1995) 'Education for citizenship and the problem of identity in post-modern political culture' in AHIER, J. and ROSS, A. (Eds) (1995) *The Social Subjects Within the Curriculum: Children's Social Learning in the National Curriculum*, London, Falmer Press.

GOLBY, M. (1986) 'Microcomputers and curriculum change' in DAVIS, R. *et al.* (Eds) *The Infant School: Past, Present and Future*, Bedford Way Papers 27, London, University of London Insitutute of Education.

GOLBY, M. (1988) 'Traditions in primary education' in CLARKSON, M. (Ed) *Emerging Issues in Primary Education*, London, Falmer Press.

GOLBY, M. (1994) 'After Dearing: A critical review of the Dearing report', *The Curriculum Journal*, **5**, 1.

GRAMSCI, A. (1971) *Selections From the Prison Notebooks of Antonio Gramsci*, (edited by HOARE, Q. and SMITH, G.) London, Lawrence & Wishart.

HALL, S. (1991) 'Reading Gramsci' in SIMON, R. (Ed) *Gramsci's Political Thought*, London, Lawrence and Wishart.

HALL, S., HELD, D. and McGREW, T. (1992) *Modernity and its Futures*, Oxford, Polity Press and the Open University Press.

HARGREAVES, A. (1994) *Changing Teachers, Changing Times: Teachers' Work and Culture in the Postmodern Age*, London, Cassell.

HARTLEY, D. (1994a) 'Mixed messages in education policy: Sign of the times?', *British Journal of Education Studies*, **XXXX11**, 3.

HARTLEY, D. (1994b) 'Confusion in teacher education: A postmodern condition?', *Journal of Teacher Education*, **19**, 4 and 5.

HARVEY, D. (1992) *The Condition of Postmodernity*, Oxford, Blackwell.

HILL, D. (1991) 'What the radical right is doing to teacher education: A radical left response', *Multicultural Teaching*, **10**, 3.

KEARNEY, R. (1988) *The Wake of Imagination: Toward a Postmodern Culture*, Minneapolis, MN, University of Minnesota Press.

KELLY, A.V. (1995) *Education and Democracy: Principles and Practices*, London, Chapman.

LACLAU, E. (1993) 'Democracy by installements' in WILKS, S. (Ed) *Talking About Tomorrow: A New Radical Politics*, London, Pluto Press.

LATHER, P. (1992) 'Postmodernism and the human sciences' in KVALE, S. (Ed) *Psychology and Postmodernism*, London, Sage Publications.

LIPMAN, M. (1991) *Thinking in Education*, London, Cambridge University Press.

LYOTARD, L. (1992) *The Postmodern Condition:: A Report on Knowledge*, Manchester, Manchester University Press.

MACKENZIE, R. (1983) 'Return to Oxfordshire': *E204 Purpose and Planning in the Curriculum*, Milton Keynes, Open University Press.

MACKENZIE, R. (1995) 'The pitfalls Blair will have to avoid', *Parliamentary Brief*, **4**, 1.

McROBBIE, A. (1994) 'Feminism, postmodernism and the real me' in PERRYMAN, M. (Ed) *Altered States: Postmodernism, Politics, Culture*, London, Lawrence and Wishart.

MARSHALL, S. (1963) *An Experiment In Education*, London, Cambridge University Press.

MARSHALL, S. (1970) *An Experiment in Education*, Cambridge, Cambridge University Press.

MOUFFE, C. (1993) 'A radical left project?' in WILKS, S. (Ed) *Talking About Tomorrow: A New Radical Politics*, London, Pluto Press.

NCC (1993) *Moral and Spiritual Education: A Discussion Paper*, York, National Curriculum Council.

NIAS, J. (1989) *Primary Teachers Talking — A Study of Teaching as Work*, London, Routledge.

OFSTED (1994) *Spiritual, Moral, Social and Cultural Development: A Discussion Paper*, London, DFE.

O'SULLIVAN, N. (1993) 'Political integration, the limited state, and the philosophy of postmodernism', *Political Studies*.

PETERS, R.S. (Ed) (1969) *Perspectives on Plowden*, London, Routledge.

POLLARD, A. (1990) 'The aims of primary school teachers' in PROCTOR, N. (Ed) *The Aims of Education and The National Curriculum*, London, Falmer Press.

POLLARD, A. (1996) *An Introduction to Primary Education*, London, Cassell.

POLLARD, A., BROADFOOT, P., CROLL, P., OSBORN, M. and ABBOTT, D. (1994) *Changing English Primary Schools? The Impact of the Education Reform Act at Key Stage One*, London, Cassell.

POLLARD, A., OSBORN, M., ABBOT, D., BROADFOOT, P. and CROLL, P. (1993) 'Balancing priorities: Children and curriculum in the nineties' in CAMPBELL, J. (Ed) *Breadth and Balance in the Primary Curriculum*, London, Falmer Press.

POLLARD, A. and TANN, S. (1992) *Reflective Teaching in the Primary School*, London, Cassell.

RANSON, S. (1994) *Towards the Learning Society*, London, Cassell.

READ, H. (1961) *Education Through Art*, London, Faber.

RICHARDS, C. (1982) 'Primary education: 1974–80' in RICHARDS, C. (Ed) *New Directions in Primary Education*, London, Falmer Press.

RODGERS, V. (1968) *The Social Subjects in English Education*, London, Heinemann.

ROSS, A. (1995a) 'The rise and fall of the social subjects in the curriculum' in AHIER, J. and ROSS, A. (Eds) (1995) *The Social Subjects Within the Curriculum Children's Social Learning in the National Curriculum*, London, Falmer Press.

ROSS, A. (1995b) 'Children in an economic world: Young children learning in a consumerist and post-industrial society' in SIRAJ-BLATCHFORD, J. and SIRAJ-BLATCHFORD, I. (Eds) (1995) *Educating the Whole Child: Cross Curricular skills, Themes and Dimensions*, Buckingham, Open University Press.

ROSZAK, T. (1981) *Person/Planet*, London, Granada.

SHARP, R. and GREEN, A. (1975) *Education and Social Control*, London, Routledge & Kegan Paul.

SILCOCK, P. (1993) 'Towards a new progressivism in primary school education', *Educational Studies*, **19**, 1.

SILVER, H. (1983) *Education as History*, London, Methuen.

SIMON, B. (1981) 'The primary school revolution: Myth or reality?' in SIMON, B. and WILLCOCKS, J. (Eds) *Research and Practice in the Primary Classroom*, London, Routledge and Kegan Paul.

SIMON, B. and CHITTY, C. (1993) *SOS: Save Our Schools*, London, Routledge.

SIRAJ-BLATCHFORD, J. (1995) 'Little citizens: Helping children to help each other' in SIRAJ-BLATCHFORD, J. and SIRAJ-BLATCHFORD, I. (Eds (1995) *Educating the Whole Child: Cross Curricular skills, Themes and Dimensions*, Buckingham, Open University Press.

SMART, B. (1993) *Postmodernity*, London, Routledge.

SMYTH, J. (Ed) (1987) *Educating Teachers: Changing the Nature of Pedagogical Knowledge*, London, Falmer Press.

SQUIRES, J. (Ed) (1993) *Principled Positions*, London, Lawrence & Wishart.

TATE, N. (1996) 'To the lighthouse', Platform, *The Times Educational Supplement*, 1 March, p. 19.

THOMPSON, K. (1992) 'Social pluralism and post-modernity' in HALL, S., HELD, D. and McGREW, T. (1992) *Modernity and its Futures*, Oxford, Polity Press and the Open University Press.

USHER, R. and EDWARDS, R. (1994) *Postmodernism and Education*, London, Routledge.

VYGOTSKY, L.S. (1962) *Thought and Language*, Cambridge, MA, Harvard University Press.

VYGOTSKY, L.S. (1978) *Mind in Society: The Development of Higher Psychlogical Processes*, Cambridge, MA, Harvard University Press.

WILKIN, M. (1993) 'Initial training as case of postmodern development: some implications for mentoring' in McINTYRE, D., HAGGER, H. and WILKIN, M. (Eds) *Mentoring: Perspectives on School Based Teacher Education*, London, Kogan Page.

WILLIAMS, R. (1976) *Keywords: A Vocabulary of Culture and Society*, Glasgow, Fontana Collins.

WILLIAMS, R. (1983) *Towards 2000*, London, Chatto and Windus.

WOODS, P. (1995) *Creative Teachers in Primary Schools*, Buckingham, Open University Press.

ZEICHNER, K. (1995) 'Research on teacher thinking and different views of reflective practice in teaching and teacher education' in CARLGEN, I., HANDAL, G. and VAAGE, S. (Eds) *Teachers' Minds and Actions: Research on Teachers' Thinking and Practice*, London, Falmer Presss.

2 Making Sense with Stories

Mim Hutchings

This chapter focuses on how story-telling can be viewed as a bridge between oracy and literacy and how this relates to the Revised Statutory Orders for English. It starts by considering how the orders might lead teachers into making judgments about children without considering the social context in which learning takes place. The chapter then reviews one approach to supporting children in recognizing the relationship between listening, speaking, reading and writing through their diverse experiences of stories. The next section considers how a wider view of the contribution of story to learning can be integrated with the demands of the new statutory orders. Finally it looks at some of the principles that might inform our work in the classroom.

It begins with the opening of a story by Elroy and Len, age 8.

Elroy:	Yeah man. A wicky wicky. This is how the story begins and my friend Len will tell you all about it.
Len:	You mean Leonardo.
Elroy:	No way.
Len:	Uh um, OK then Raphael, this is part two of the
Chorus:	*Teenage Mutant Hero Turtles.*
Elroy:	Not to mention Splinter, right?
Len:	Um these Teenage Turtles was in their likkle um likkle cave, well likkle sewer right. Likkle part of the sewer and they was walking down to see if everything was alright. When they see this computer and when they looked on the computer, they pressed a button on it and there's a hole in the wall and it opened up. So, they went through and it was sort of electric all around them. So they started to walk down the road.
Elroy:	Know what I mean.

This short extract illustrates two close friends playing with a favourite TV story. It is the kind of activity often observed in children at play. The ground rules for their elaborate game are directly linked to the TV series it originates from.

Pause for a moment before reading on and consider the following extracts from the Programmes of Study, Key Stage 2 Speaking and Listening:

— Pupils should be taught to listen carefully and recall and re-present important features of a television programme.
— Pupils' appreciation and use of standard English should be developed by involvement with others in activities that, through their content and purpose, demand the range of grammatical constructions and vocabulary characteristic of spoken standard English. They should be taught to speak with clear diction and appropriate intonation.

What judgments would you make about these two boys? Perhaps you concluded that these boys don't know the grammatical constructions of standard English or even what a sentence is. Or maybe that some serious attempt should be made to correct their diction. You might also have thought that this can't possibly be considered a good example of recalling and re-presenting a TV programme, at least not when thinking of the National Curriculum. Such judgments operate continually in the classroom. Frequently based on partial and insubstantial evidence they remind us that our professional decisions are driven by values, prejudices and hidden assumptions both within ourselves and throughout the apparently bland directives of the National Curriculum. Listening to these boys most teachers would enjoy their imaginative play with language yet recognize, this is not educational discourse. Teachers would be keen to encourage these boys to use their knowledge and experience in order to draw them closer to the literary models that are a part of life and learning in the classroom. 'Although schools are places with their own special kinds of knowledge and their own ways of using language, and their own power relationships, they do not stand outside the wider society. And learners have social identities which affect how they act, and how other people act, in the classroom.' (Mercer, 1995, p. 96).

The Revised Statutory Orders for English represents one such influence from the wider society that has to be considered. The document as a whole leaves the reader with a sense that English must be boring and mechanical and in practical terms that it should be all grammar and spelling tests. Cox (1995) suggests that 'this peculiar document opens doors. Most restrictions in the 1993 and 1994 drafts have been removed. What is left is often bare, boring and brief, but good teachers are allowed to develop their own initiatives' (p. 168). The document contains little to stimulate and excite teachers but nevertheless we have to work with it and that is the subject of this chapter.

As anticipated, the documents reduce English to bland basics. However, it is this blandness that offers teachers the scope for imaginative inventiveness in implementing the Orders. This does not mean there are no problems. For example, confronted with Elroy and Len and their imaginative reworking of a TV programme what should be done about their use of non-standard forms of English? Listening to their skilful combining of a variety of dialects from the original TV programme, peer group and locality, I remember that the way we speak is tightly tied into our social, cultural and individual view of who we are. The findings of the SCAA investigations into Children's Use of Spoken Standard

English (Hudson and Holmes, 1995, p. 9) remind us that both gender and the age of pupils are part of this complex network, 'more girls than boys use SSE'. They also comment that 'the effect of age is rather interesting, and somewhat unexpected from an educational point of view'. With '15-year-olds producing *fewer* speakers of SSE than the 11-year-olds'. Professional judgment supported by sociolinguistic research such as Labov (1972) Trudghill (1978) and Edwards (1983) informs us that the use of dialect does not stop anyone expressing their ideas clearly. That, the assumed prestige of spoken standard English is a so-cially constructed notion that makes little sense in relation to the development of childrens' abilities to think and learn. Cox (1995) recognizes this in his objections to the presence of spoken standard English in the Level descrip-tions 'if this is to be tested, many intelligent working class children who speak vividly and forcibly will have difficulty proceeding beyond Level 6, while a dull middle-class child will easily manage an exceptional performance' (p. 160).

A practical starting point for working beyond such a narrow perception of language and its use is to review the decisions that need to be made to ensure that Elroy, Len and their classmates are drawn into the culture of liter-ate practices in the classroom. And, consider how the English documents might help or hinder that process. I intend to examine how story-telling might provide a framework for supporting children's learning and relate this to the Revised Statutory Orders for English.

There are two main reasons for choosing story-telling. The first is that stories have always been important to the education of children, among the things that children are expected to do in school is read, write and listen to stories. It has always struck me as surprising that they are not so frequently asked to tell stories. Whilst the centrality of narrative to the education process is recognized through numerous references to stories, the oral aspects of tell-ing are less frequently focused on. The second is the way in which story-telling can be used as a bridge between oracy and literacy. In order to learn to read and write children need to manage larger units of speech than is usual in their conversation, moving from telling stories to reading and writing can help children rehearse and understand some of the similarities and differences between spoken and written English (POS Key Stage 2 Standard English and Language Study, a). For bilingual children it offers the opportunity of extend-ing the comparison to differences and similarities between languages. As Gregory (1996) suggests 'stories, then act as mediators of language and culture to children entering a new world in the classroom' (p. 117). Telling stories is one way that the interrelated nature of the modes of language can be woven into rehearsing, planning, drafting in a way which draws on children's existing language skills. The introduction to the programmes of study recognizes that 'pupils' abilities should be developed within an integrated programme of speak-ing and listening, reading and writing'. However, the separation of talk, read-ing and writing within the documents tends to mask the contribution each makes to the other. The primary focus becomes the differences. Through being told stories, reworking them orally and finally writing them children are reminded that essentially it is language they are working with whatever the mode. The focus then becomes the similarities between oral and written language followed by the specific differences needed to convey the oral text into the written. None of these differences or similarities are spelt out in any detail in the documentation. What do they look like to Neil and Lakshmi, age 7 in retelling and writing a version of *The Wolf and The Three Girls* (source Calvino, 1987)?

Neil and Lakshmi, oral version

One day there was three kids and they was grown up and they left home because they was very big now. One day they had a letter. The letter says their Mum was sick. Then the girl got one cake, then another, then another and that makes three and three loaves of bread. She went to her mum's with the present because she was ill. She was walking when a wolf popped out and said,
'Where are you going in this hot weather?'
'I'm going to see my mum. She's ill.'
The wolf said,
'Give me those cakes or I'll eat you up.'

The printed text of the oral version loses the performance elements such as the intonation, variation of pace, gestures and expressions for which punctuation is no real substitute yet it reveals how closely it parallels the final book version:

Neil and Lakshmi, written version

One day there was three girls and their mum sent them a letter because she was ill. One of the three girls set off to go and see how she was. She took bread and cakes. On the way she met a wolf and the wolf said,
'Where are you going in this hot weather?'
'To visit my mum because she is ill.'
'Give me those cakes or else I'll gobble you up.'

In the spoken version it is possible to hear the two children rehearsing and developing the original story especially in this section from the middle of the same story.

Neil and Lakshmi, oral version

And he went,
'Give me that or else I'll eat you up.'
But the wolf was a bit fulled up and he said
'Ahh, I'll have a little, give me those cakes or else I'll eat you up.'
The girl chucked the basket, no picked up a cake and chucked it.

The wolf got it in his mouth and he went, 'mmmm' and he ate it all
up. There was nails in it and he went,
'awwww, I'll get you back one day for this.'
The wolf went to the mum's house and gobbled her up and put on
her nice juicy hat and everything. Then the girl come and the wolf
said,
'Hi de daughter, what do you want?'
The daughter said,
'I want to see you. Ooh, how comes you look so different?'
'Oh, oh, I feel sick that's why.'

The written version of the same section looked like this:

The wolf said,
'Give me those those cakes or I'll gobble you up.'
The girl chucked one of the cakes and said,
'Here catch.'
The wolf caught the cake in his mouth. The wolf screamed,
'awww'.
It was full of nails. He said,
'One day I'll get you back.'
The wolf went to the Mum's house and he gobbled her up. After he
put on her nightie and got into bed. The girl came to the mum's house
and said,
'Hello Mum you look different.'
'I know my dear because I am ill. Come a bit closer.'

The told sections retain, even in print, some of the sense of vitality that was
characteristic of many of the stories told by the children which is not so
evident in the written versions.

The oral sections contain some examples of the differences between spoken
and written language which are omitted or revised in the written form

— hesitations: ummm
— reworkings: The girl chucked the basket, no picked up a cake and
  chucked it.
— more colloquial expressions: a wolf popped out, and, Ooh, how comes
  you look so different?

All these are features of the difference between speech and writing that children need to understand in order to become effective writers. Typically the
spoken version has a tendency to use clauses such as 'The wolf went to the
mum's house and gobbled her up and put on her nice juicy hat and everything.' The clauses are linked by the use of and. However, because it is a story
and therefore more continuous than conversation some subordinating clauses

are also evident for example 'She went to her mum's with the present because she was ill. She was walking when a wolf popped out.' Interestingly these are not retained within the written version but here indicate that Neil and Lakshmi are beginning to recognize that large chunks of text achieve integration through the use of such grammatical devices. Neil and Lakshmi are obviously confident in shaping the start of the story and using repetition which is essential to the style of the story. They are using appropriate tenses past, present and future most of the time.

The general tendency is to emphasize the differences between spoken language and written, thereby seeming almost to see writing as separate from talking. Undoubtedly there are many examples of genres of writing that are very different for example it would be rare to hear a recipe given orally. Czerniewska (1992) suggests that a more helpful approach to understanding the differences and similarities is to make functional comparisions that recognize how some forms of writing are closer to speech than others. That, the differences become increasingly apparent when you compare two very different forms for example a conversation and an essay. Writing is most usually seen as having a greater degree of integration than speech. In Neil and Lakshmi's written version of the story this is achieved through the use of cohesive ties such as and, because, after, and the use of pronouns such as she, her, he. Writing is often talked about as being more syntactically complex. Speech as more fragmentary, containing the hesitations and repetitions evident in Neil and Lakshmi's oral version of *The Wolf and the Three Girls*. Czerniewska (1992) gives some helpful examples of the similarities in speech and writing:

Integration	**Fragmentation**
school textbook	shopping list
prepared lecture	informal chat

Returning to the sections of story quoted above it is possible to see how story-telling becomes one of the bridges between speech and writing. Although the told versions retained some of the fragmentary elements of speech, syntactically they generally contained more of the elements of writing and a greater degree of integration. As would be expected of 7-year-old children they are more skilled speakers than writers. Their growing knowledge of the features of sustained pieces of text is shown in the oral versions but not in the written. The written versions tend to concentrate on short sentences with few subordinate clauses and a narrow range of cohesive ties for example, and, because, when. Story-telling in this instance shows how oral and written language share the same underlying structures and might be used to support each other.

When I first started working with children on storytelling I had the idea that there might be some elements of oral drafting similar to the drafting process in writing which is exemplified by writers such as Graves (1983) and mentioned in the programmes of study for writing. And, that this could be used to extend pupils' control in telling stories. However with wider experience of working with children and story tellers I came to understand that there are major differences in the way we rehearse for story telling and prepare to write a story. The evidence I collected suggested that there is planning as we tell and retell stories but not all telling requires the formal attention to conventions that are needed in writing. Betty Rosen (1988) suggests why this might be the case, 'It is my view that the dynamic of listening to a story being told somehow amalgamates the two processes of receiving and reflecting upon the material' (p. 72). In this case an additional layer was added in that the children followed up the listening by retelling the story before writing it. Thus the tape became their draft or rehearsal for the writing. The told versions provided me with an insight into the extent of the children's potential as storytellers and language users that would not have been evident in their written work or other kinds of talk used in the classoom, for example, group discussions. We are aware that children (and many adults!) are better talkers than writers, yet we rarely provide opportunities that support children in talking like writers. These two children from a special needs class within a mainstream school surprised us with the level of their achievement and were justifiably proud of the book they produced and could read to the class. The story telling activities had empha-sized their strengths as language users rather than their 'problems'.

This example was indicative of the kind of response from a range of classes and children. The catalyst for all the children's storying was being told a range of stories then allowing them the opportunity to record a story of their own. Initially the stories told by the children were often retellings of my story but as they grew in confidence they selected their own stories. Increasingly the children used the sessions to experiment with a range of stories including stories based on jokes and personal experience. Stories were told in the lan-guages and dialects of the locality. The making of tapes and books for the school led to lively discussion of appropriate content and language within personal tapes and for a wider audience. Most usually the sources of their stories were favourite books, TV programmes or films. The recordings pro-vided the basis for my understanding of how the final stories were shaped by the language and form of the original sources. The regulation beginning, middle and end of the Programmes of Study is too narrow a definition of narrative structure for the range of stories told by children. For example, one story which originated from a horror film contained the spiralling action which was evident in the original. It began with a simple act and went through a series of increasingly violent sequences, playing on the fears that the horribly unex-pected can happen in stories. The rising action was expressed through a series of short clauses each linked by conjunctions:

Knock Out Ginger **told by Mike age 11**
It's your turn to knock now.
Knock, knock, knock.
And the door came crashing down.
Bang.

Soon they all went in.
They came to this spiral staircase, going down, so they went down it.

Where the original version was a traditional story such as *Jack and the Beanstalk* the final version mirrored the source often by following on with a sequel.

Jack and the Beanstalk — The sequel told by Keith, age 11 opens with:
Time had passed since Jack had killed the Giantess's husband, the main Giant. For this the Giantess had let Jack stay with her. One day there was a knock at the door.

Children's personal experiences of story shape their theories of what is an appropriate narrative structure for the particular story they are telling. Thus, the traditional story had a conventional beginning, middle and end. The story based on the film was a series of episodes with a gruesome ending. The story based on the TV series quoted at the start of the chapter amalgamated several episodes of the series with no distinctions drawn between the start of one section and the next. The common element was their lively inventiveness in experimenting with their knowledge of the conventions of story. This context provided an opportunity for the children to show what they could achieve and for me a chance to observe and describe their achievements. It is an example of what Fisher (1995) calls 'unconscious planning' needed because 'young children learn how to perform tasks, before they are able to understand what they are doing and why' (p. 33). It was also a reminder of how the demands of implementing a narrow literary view of narrative, implicit in the programmes of study, could close down opportunities for developing children as learners. The stories told by the children showed a clear understanding of how to match the shape of a story to the appropriate language in order to convey precisely the tone and mood of the tale. They also illustrated how links can be made between classroom learning and what happens outside the school. In all the activities associated with story-telling one of the most noticeable changes was the growth in confidence and self-esteem of the children I worked with. This was marked by an increasing willingness to participate and a desire to prepare stories to tell or write for other children. For example, Grace (aged 8) in the time she spent in the story-telling group moved from being unwilling, nervous, disorganized and disruptive to being confident enough to keep the nursery class enthralled with her story. Many of the children I worked with were struggling to make sense of school and what it might offer them. Story telling seemed to offer them a chance to draw on their knowledge and experience which enhanced their achievement and self-esteem. Fisher (1995) sums up the relationship 'children value themselves as learners to the degree that they have been valued. To focus on achievement in learning without also focusing on building self-esteem is only to half-educate a child' (p. 124). The National Curriculum document, with its heavy focus on content and skills, seems to suggest only half of the picture. The other half needs to be built into the way we work with children to develop them as independent and critical learners who draw on their rich and diverse linguistic experience.

What is it about story-telling that makes it such an important part of developing children as learners? Earlier I said that we seem to acknowledge the centrality of narrative to education, why is this the case? Bruner (1990) suggests that storying has a fundamental role in ordering and developing thinking or framing. 'Framing provides a means of "constructing" a world, of characterizing its flow, of segmenting events within that world, and so on. If we were not able to do such framing, we would be lost in a murk of chaotic experience and probably would not have survived as a species in any case' (p. 56). This suggests that story-telling is part of the routine of our lives whether it is telling an anecdote, watching a favourite soap, going to the shops or day dreaming. In making sense of our world we participate in and tell stories. Thus if story is seen to be part of our everyday events and actions it should also be viewed as an explicit resource for intellectual activity. It is this sense that everyday experiences and the literary are not so far apart that makes it so important in the classroom. Perhaps it is through this understanding of story that we start to see scientific explanations and history as part of the way we construct the stories of the world. Or as Bruner (1990) puts it 'I have wanted to make it clear that our capacity to render experience in terms of narrative is not just child's play, but an instrument for making meaning that dominates much of our culture — from soliloquies at bedtime to the weighing of testimony in our legal system' (p. 97).

A major part of this chapter has been devoted to exploring the way in which story-telling can help to introduce children to the culture of literate practice in the classroom. The opportunities for personal and intellectual development and, the development of crucial language skills have been looked at through the stories that children told and wrote. At this point it is worth summarizing some of the key elements which contribute to the relevance of story telling in the classroom:

Personal
- giving enjoyment
- developing the imagination
- offering ways of considering identity, making sense of experiences; understanding fears, conflicts, predicaments

Learning
- giving access to new ideas and knowledge
- developing the understanding of concepts
- developing understanding of hidden meanings and values

Language
- experience of the shape of story
- understanding words and the structure of language
- control and experimentation in conveying points of view and meaning

Clearly these are also the elements which underpin the use of narrative within a broad range of contexts in the classroom. In this instance the oral language has provided the foundation for the development of literacy. Talking, listening, reading and writing are being promoted simultaneously through interaction between the language modes. Although the English document starts with a recognition of the interrelated nature of language the subsequent division of the Programmes of Study into listening and speaking, reading and writing masks the common themes. The elements relating to learning and language listed above appear scattered throughout the documents. Personal development, as with the aspects of self-esteem discussed earlier, are absent from this cold and bureaucratic document. However, picking through the document it is possible to find the following threads linked to language and learning in Key Stage 2:

Range
Speaking and Listening
• reading aloud, telling and enacting stories
Reading
Pupils' reading should include texts with:
• challenging subject matter that broadens perspectives and extends thinking
• more complex narrative structures and sustained ideas
Writing
They should be taught to use the characteristics of different kinds of writing

Key Skills
Speaking and Listening
Pupils should be taught to organize what they want to say, and to use vocabulary and syntax that enables the communication of more complex meanings
Reading
They should be encouraged to respond imaginatively to the plot, characters, ideas, vocabulary, and organization of language in literature
Writing
Pupils' should be given opportunities to plan, draft and improve their work

Standard English and Language Study
Speaking and Listening
They should also be given opportunities to develop their understanding of the similarities and differences between the written and spoken forms of standard English
Reading
Pupils' should be introduced to the organizational, presentational features of different types of text
Writing
Pupils' should be given opportunities to develop understanding of the grammar of complex sentences, including clauses and phrases.

Compiling a list such as this highlights the artificial boundaries that could be created between oracy and literacy from this sporadic and disorganized curriculum. Children learn to read and write by talking and listening and making sense of the forms of language they will learn to read and write in school. Much of the activity in classrooms focuses on children making and using language to learn. I hope that I have illustrated that story-telling is one way of planning a classroom context which takes account of the integrated nature of language use.

Returning to Elroy, Len and their classmates and the judgments that may be made on the basis of the current statements about standard English, the approach that I have been describing is largely based on the assumption that using children's current knowledge about language provides the basis for extending the varities of language(s) they use. This follows the tradition used by many teachers involved in the National Oracy Project for enhancing and developing children's knowledge about language and discussed in Bains (1992). To some extent this is also encouraged within the general requirements of the document 'the richness of dialects and other languages can make an important contribution to pupils' knowledge and understanding of standard English. Where appropriate, pupils should be encouraged to make use of their understanding and skills in other languages when learning English.' However, the heavy emphasis on spoken standard English brings to the surface overt discrimination in favour of those children arriving in school already speaking spoken standard English. The problem is that the document shows little understanding of real children and the social and cultural identities they bring to learning. From the framework suggested a number of principles emerge as important:

— recognize how children's linguistic skills and cultural knowledge can become part of the learning process;
— use stories that stem from children's experience;
— offer opportunities for children to tell, discuss and reform stories;
— tell (and read) stories that have a strong storyline, if the language is difficult make sure it is clear and memorable, for example, through rhyme and repetition;
— by linking spoken and written language we help children recognize the relationship between the two;
— retelling stories can give important information on progress in language.

Finally, how far do these documents hinder us in providing a high quality education for children? I hope through this exploration of story-telling it will be apparent that I believe that they will only hinder us if we allow the bureaucratic and mechanistic ethos dominate the way we implement the content.

References

Bains, R. (Ed) (1992) *Looking into Language*, London, Hodder & Stoughton.
Bruner, J. (1990) *Acts of Meaning*, Cambridge, MA, Harvard University Press.

CALVINO, I. (1987) *Italian Folk Tales*, Penguin Folklore Library, London, Penguin.

Cox, B. (1995) *Cox on The Battle For the English Curriculm*, London, Hodder & Stoughton.

CZERNIEWSKA, P. (1992) *Learning About Writing, The Early Years, Language in Education*, Oxford Blackwell.

DFE (1995) *English in the National Curriculum*, London, HMSO.

EDWARDS, V. (1983) *Language in Multicultural Classrooms*, London, Batsford Academic Publishers.

FISHER, R. (1995) Teaching Children to Learn, Cheltenham, Stanley Thornes.

GRAVES, D. (1983) *Writing: Teachers and Children at Work*, Heinnemann, Portsmouth, NH.

GREGORY, E. (1996) *Making Sense of a New World, Learning to Read in a Second Language*, London, PCP.

HUDSON, R. and HOLMES, J. (1995) *Children's Use of Spoken Standard English*, London, School Curriculum and Assessment Authority.

LABOV, W. (1972) *Language in the Inner City: Studies in the Black English Vernacular*, Oxford Blackwell.

MERCER, N. (1995) *The Guided Construction of Knowledge, Talk amongst Teachers and Learners*, Clevedon, Multilingual Matters.

ROSEN, B. (1988) *And None of It Was Nonsense, The Power of Storytelling in School*, London, Mary Glasgow Publications.

TRUDGHILL, P. (Ed) (1978) *Sociolinguistic Patterns in British English*, London, Edward Arnold.

3 Beginnings, Middles and Ends: Whose Realities?

John Gulliver

Classroom Realities, Curriculum Questions

Human beings, it is widely recognized, have the facility to live in multiple realities. The most prominent, it has been claimed, is the reality of everyday life, the privileged position of which '. . . entitles it to the designation of *paramount reality*' (Berger and Luckman, 1966, p. 35, my emphasis). One might assume that children share this general human capacity, and that to them everyday life is likewise central. Of this life, the classroom occupies a substantial part. This chapter is concerned with whether, for young children, the curricular world of the classroom coincides with their realities beyond it, and with how ideologies of curriculum and teaching, including those underpinning National Curriculum English, as it has evolved through the years of the Dearing Review, sustain the links or drives wedges between them.

Referring to infant classrooms which he studied, one writer has indicated that most of what happened within them was arranged or allowed to happen by the teacher (King, 1978, p. 10). Children, King claimed, learned to share their teachers' definitions of classroom reality, not only in relation to its social demands, but also with regard to 'the story worlds of reading, the writing worlds of news and story, and the world of number and mathematics' (*ibid.*, p. 34). In short, they adopted their teachers' curricular worlds of meaning, as well as their social worlds.

In the light of other research, one might want to temper King's claims. Doyle (1986), for example, has argued for classroom order and the demands of learning activities to be regarded as matters achieved *with* students. Nevertheless, the substance of King's point stands. Even if their power is incomplete, the teacher's role in defining classroom realities is substantial. There is nothing in this to occasion surprise. Nor, in principle, should it cause regret, for one of the functions of education is to offer to learners conceptions of reality which have claims to be of value.

Nevertheless, the relative ease with which pupils, and especially the very young, may embrace what they are offered places an awesome responsibility on teachers and those who help to shape teachers' realities for the worlds created and explored within classrooms. It raises questions of many kinds.

Some, for example, relate to the means by which teachers establish their versions of reality within their spheres of work. Others involve the nature, sources, justifications and worth of these realities. The former relate to pedagogy, the latter to curriculum. Common to all are matters of teaching ideologies, which, for this chapter, I shall take to be:

> . . . connected set(s) of systematically related beliefs and ideas about what are felt to be the essential features of teaching. (Sharp and Green, 1975, p. 68)

I shall be concerned with the consequences of such beliefs and ideas for the worlds of meaning children inhabit and explore in school, and, in particular, with how statutory requirements may combine with practices deeply rooted in teaching ideology to ensure that, even in that allegedly most child-centred theatre of education, the English infant classroom, what children explore within school may impinge on their realities beyond it at no more than a superficial level.

I shall consider these matters in relation to a brief recently observed episode from classroom life. It involved a student in the initial year of a BEd course, undertaking her first teaching practice, for which I was her supervising tutor. It related especially to an activity she had planned and carried out with some children from a reception class. The activity called for book-making and story-writing, and highlighted 'the front page, (the) title of (the) book, and *the beginning, middle and end* to the story' (Sally, 1993a, my emphasis).

The collection of data relating to the episode was governed by a primary concern to support the student's professional development. Hence, it consists of my own running notes, photocopies of the work of a child on whom my attention focused and the student's own notes and subsequent comments. Illustrations from the child's work and references to the student's notes and comments are made with their kind permission.

Beginnings, Middles and Ends: A Classroom Episode

An infant classroom. A dozen 5-year-olds, part of a larger reception class, split in order to give the student, who I will call Sally, although that is not her real name, an opportunity to work on her own with a group of children. The children are sitting in threes and fours around small tables, busily writing, drawing and talking. The room is calm. From time to time the children take what they are doing to show to Sally. More frequently, she approaches them, easing herself into the tiny chairs alongside them to talk with them about their work. Even though she has known them only for a fortnight, her rapport with the children is well founded.

Sally has carefully worked out with the class's regular teacher what she wants to do with the children throughout the session. Building on *James and the Jungle*, a picture-book well-known to the class, she is attempting a 'story-book writing lesson' (Sally, 1993c). She has already re-read the story to the children, 'emphasizing different parts which the author had included, funny parts, parts where James was mad, naughty parts etc.'. She has shown them a blank book that she has put together with sugar paper, and has elicited its need for words, pictures and a cover picture to make it a proper book. Further to the children's suggestions, she has emphasized that a story 'needs a beginning, a middle and an end' (same place):

> Something happens to start a story; like with *James and the Jungle* it was about gardening; a middle, something exciting, naughty, funny, sad or scary; and then an ending, happy or sad. (same place)

The children have made their own versions of the blank books, folding the sugar paper already prepared for them, binding it with brightly coloured wool. Each book has its space for a cover picture and specified pages for its beginning, middle and end. Sally has left what the books are to be about open, a course she feels to be more interesting to the children.

By the time of my arrival, most of the children have made front covers and completed the first page for their books. Sally talks mainly with the children as individuals. From time to time, however, she breaks off to speak encouragingly to the group as a whole. She reminds the children of the need for beginnings, middles and ends. She emphasizes the happy ending to *James and the Jungle* and the possibilities for such conclusions to the children's stories.

I sit beside one of the girls, beside whom there is a (tiny) vacant seat. She tells me that her name is Claire and allows me to watch what she is doing. Her front cover is complete (figure 3.1). On a sheet of white paper, roughly the size of a paperback novel, it consists mainly of a number of pencil drawings: some cats; a dog; a zebra (whose apparently incongruous presence Sally later attributes to the *James and the Jungle* book); and a rainbow arching over the right-hand page-top. Most of them are coloured in crayon. The rainbow has been done in blue, purple, red, orange, black, yellow, brown and green, laid out as segments of an arc rather than concentrically. The dog is black and the zebra blue and green. One cat, larger than the rest, is a felt-tipped vivid green and yellow. The others are uncoloured. A blue sky is crayoned beneath the rainbow. In the top, left-hand, part of the page, Claire has written 'day book' in carefully formed letters. Sally has helped her to paste the work onto the front of her sugar-paper book.

The first, the 'beginning' of the story, is also complete and stuck in (figure 3.2). At its head, spread across the paper, is Claire's writing: 'DAewwenTHOIi day'. Beneath it, Sally has transcribed Claire's text conventionally, adding a possessive: 'My daddy went on holiday'. Claire's drawing, with lightly pencilled outline, is of her daddy. He stands in ski-trousers and top on skis, holding ski-sticks complete with straps in gloved and fingered hands. He wears a tall

Figure 3.1: Claire's front cover

ski-hat, topped by a pom-pom. His goggled face smiles broadly. His face and hat are lightly crayoned in brown. All else, including the snow, is lightly shaded in pink and red.

As I sit with her, Claire is busy with the next page. She has drawn a rectangular shape, roughly twice as long as it is broad, horizontally on the page. Within in, filling the available space, is a figure, front on. Except for a prominent blob in the middle of the torso, only the head is detailed. The face is unsmiling. 'It's my daddy's daddy in his grave', she says.

Claire takes the drawing to Sally. They are too far away for what they say to be audible. On her return, she writes 'mywwDHSDHS' at the head of the page, altering the second and fourth letters to 'n' and 'D' respectively as she goes. This she shows to Sally, who praises her and transcribes 'My daddys daddy died' under her script. Back at her seat, she copies Sally's transcription with meticulous care (figure 3.3).

Claire then begins to colour her drawing. Firstly, she covers one end, where the feet are, with purple. The other, to one side of the head, and covering one shoulder but not the head itself, she shades in red. The other side is coloured yellow, again without touching the head, but without distinction between body, arm, leg and the unfilled part of the grave. To this is added orange. Then she shades the other leg and the part of the grave next to it

Figure 3.2: First page

lightly in purple. The area beyond the head she also colours purple, but heavily. Finally she shades the head, again in purple, but lightly, rapidly and in looping movements quite unlike the horizontals and verticals she has employed previously. By now, everything within the grave, but nothing beyond it, is covered with colour (figure 3.4). Anticipating that Claire might be placing flowers on the grave, I ask about the colouring. 'My teacher likes us to colour things in in bright colours', she replies.

My knowledge of subsequent events is less extensive: there are other students with whom I need to spend time. By my return at the end of the morning, however, Claire has completed her book. On its final page she has drawn and coloured two figures, one of herself and the other of her father. Above them she has written 'BugMiWDHS', which Sally has retranscribed as: 'But my daddys still alive' (figure 3.5). The outer cover has been overlaid with sticky-back plastic film. Claire appears to be pleased, as do the other children with what they have made.

Offered Realities, Adopted Realities

Even in relation to the brief episode recounted above and its immediate antecedents, the worlds offered to the children are many. Firstly, through the

Figure 3.3: *Second page: Drawing and statement*

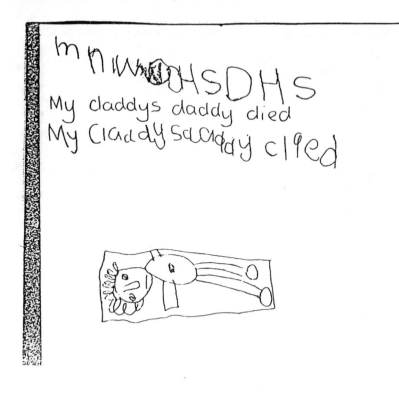

picture book, the pupils are invited into a world of narrative fiction offered through pictures and written words read aloud. Secondly, a reality is presented in which the children themselves are expected to be the constructors of narrative worlds, referred to as 'stories'. Stories are presented as discourses structured through beginnings, middles and ends, with *James and the Jungle* as an example. While earlier the characters had been highlighted, for the children's narratives the structural elements are emphasized. These are further highlighted in the booklets Sally has prepared and in the separate sheets of paper on which they work.

Drawing may be employed by the children as a means of formulating their narratives (Sally, in conversation with author). Their final presentation, however, must be primarily as verbal, written, objects. The attention given to their transcription, and then to their translation into conventional orthography, signal the primacy of the written word and its conventional presentation. Colouring is undertaken after the completion of the written texts. By inference from Claire's remark about her teacher's preferences, it is allocated (although not necessarily by Sally) a decorative function, to which bright colours are suited. The resulting wholes are to be seen as books and set alongside the classroom's commercially published material.

Figure 3.4: Second page: The drawing coloured

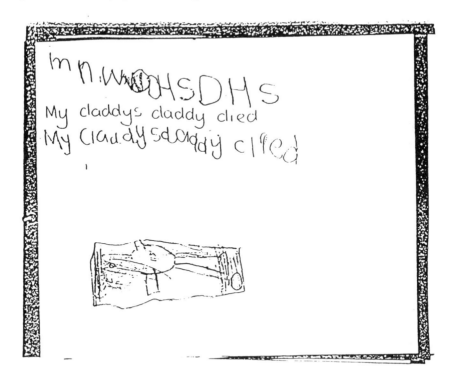

These offered realities are readily adopted by Claire and the rest of the children as their own. A dozen books are produced by a dozen pupils. Permutations are few. The most striking relate to the two areas explicitly left open. One is the content: Sally's notes, written after the session, indicate that she left '. . . what (the children) were going to write about up to them' (Sally, 1993a). A second involves the fictiveness or otherwise of the children's creations:

> Looking at all the books, there are two different sorts: fiction books and books telling a story which has happened to the child. (*ibid.*)

Claire's work falls roughly into this latter category.

In relation to this classroom at least, King's primary point stands. The children, at least at a surface level, adopt their student-teacher's version of reality.

Claire's Narrative Worlds

On the face of it, Claire has made Sally's world her own. She has made a 'book'. It contains three pieces of written text and drawings, which form the

Figure 3.5: Third page

'beginning', 'middle' and 'end' of a 'story'. She is pleased with it. Sally, too, regards the venture with satisfaction:

> I felt this activity was very worthwhile. The children did a great deal of work to complete this book and their effort really shows in the final outcome. (Sally, 1993b)

Nevertheless, further questions warrant attention. They begin with Sally's stated intention of conducting a 'story-book writing lesson' (Sally, 1993c). I shall consider two of its elements, 'story' and 'writing', taking Claire's written text (here represented conventionally) initially:

Daybook

Daddy went on holiday.
My daddy's daddy died.
But my daddy's still alive.

Neither in Sally's terms, nor in those of genre theory, is it clear that this is a story. There may be an evaluative connection between the event of the 'middle' and the final observation. The 'beginning' and 'middle' are unconnected, how-ever, except through the person of 'daddy'. Where a narrative might be defined in terms of two or more temporal clauses, thematically linked (a more technical definition than Sally's), the written text by itself does not constitute a story. The common, rather than continuing, thread is provided, not by the actors, so much as by Claire's relationship to them. It is offered in the declarative state-ments of personal experience which, according to one writer, are typical of the 'morning news genre' of children's school writing (Christie, 1987, p. 235). In the terminology offered by Martin and Rothery (1980 and 1981), the first two are recounts of experience. No significance is apparent in their order. In con-junction, their consequence is additive rather than narrative.

Yet this analysis does scant justice to Claire's status as a novice writer, or to her growing command of the possibilities of story. In the words of one investigator, 'children's first writing efforts are typically intermingled with draw-ing and talk, resulting in *multimedia creations*' (Dyson, 1988, p. 356, my emphasis). Even without a record of Claire's talk as she wrote, or protocols of her thinking, the multimedia nature of her activity is evident. Once each writ-ten statement is seen as but one element in an organic whole, then the way is open to the consideration of each of the pages as an independent construc-tion and an appreciation of the astonishing complexity of its making. In short, the starting point for a full consideration of Claire's activity as a novice writer should involve regarding the totality and interplay of her talking, drawing, colouring and writing as her text, rather than the written element alone.

Even this acknowledgement of the multimedia nature of Claire's activity is insufficient, however. One must also recognize that the composition of a story is no simple matter. Drawing on Britton's claim that it involves the crea-tion of a written world, a 'verbal object isolated from the traffic of daily exist-ence' (Britton, quoted in Dyson, 1988, p. 357), Dyson further suggests the creator of such a world must move in *multiple* (author's emphasis) worlds:

> . . . now the real world director of the unfolding imaginary plot; now, deep in that imaginary world, an actor speaking a character's words, feeling a character's emotion; then inside a remembered world, a reflective story-teller reliving past experiences; and then, a socially astute communicator adjusting words and phrases to ease interaction with real-world readers . . . (*ibid.*)

In what follows, I shall use Dyson's notion of the movement in multiple worlds that underlies the composition of imaginative texts generally, rather than in relation to written matter alone, as a framework for making inferences about the worlds that lie behind Claire's text, as it is widely conceived above.

It is enough at this point to look at Claire's first text, in which the written statement 'Daddy went on holiday' may now be seen as just the tip of an iceberg. I do not know what conversations went into its creation, or what monologues accompanied it. Nevertheless, even when the '. . . object isolated from the traffic of daily existence' is seen just in terms of her writing, drawing and colouring, the complexity of the movement in multiple worlds which went into its making begins to be visible. The intricacy of the ski gear, noted above, is a case in point. Sally states that Claire did not go on the holiday with her father. We do not know whether she saw him beforehand in his kit, or afterwards, in a photograph. We do know, however, that no representation was available when she made the drawing, except in her mind's eye. And the intricacy of her drawing is clearly visible. This, one might suggest, is to begin to see her in the role of Dyson's 'real world director of the unfolding imaginary plot'. One might examine, too, the smile on her father's face (and contrast it with the absence of this feature in her second drawing), and see in it a reflection of her movement 'deep in that imaginary world, (as) an actor . . . feeling a character's emotion'. And in her struggle to write, we might see, if not a socially astute, then at least a novitiate 'communicator adjusting words and phrases to ease interaction with real-world readers'. Viewed thus, the striking feature of Claire's text-construction lies in the multiplicity of the worlds within and between which it moves.

Whose Realities?

Focusing on Claire's second and third pages, with the grave and the two figures at their respective centres, and taking as her texts all that went into their making, I want now to consider the congruence of classroom realities as they were for Claire and for Sally in relation to their construction. To this end, I shall continue to draw on the concepts of 'reality' as employed by Berger and Luckman and by King, and of 'world' as used by Dyson. I take as my warrant the concern of these writers for the individual's articulation of experience and its relationship to the social world. While their perspectives differ, the terms 'reality' and 'worlds' they use to refer to the subjective meanings which shape individuals' actions appear to have much in common.

It will be apparent from the earlier account that Sally had defined a situation in which Claire, along with the other children, was expected to construct a second and then a third page for her book. Each page was to involve both drawing and writing and to be narratively related to its predecessor. Each drawing was to serve as the basis for the negotiated composition of a single-sentence verbal statement which Claire would then transcribe in whatever way she was able. This in its turn would be shown to Sally, who would indicate its conventional transcription. Claire was then to round things off by copying Sally's retranscription of her original statement. Taken together, the two sentences would constitute the middle and the ending of the story begun with the first page.

Behind Sally's requirements were multiple intentions. Some, spread over the project as a whole, were related to the development of book knowledge (Sally, 1993a). Hence the talk of 'cover', 'title' and 'page'. Others involved the development of an awareness of narrative structure, seen to involve beginning, middle and ending, and the ability to shape a text around it. Further to these was the expectation that, by practice, Claire would become increasingly proficient in the composition and transcription of sentences (Sally, 1993b).

Neither the situation nor the intentions behind it were random or idiosyncratic. On the contrary, they reflected four dimensions of Sally's reality as a teaching novitiate. One was the continuing life of the classroom to which she was attached. From this came a particular methodology for supporting literacy development. It required children first to draw pictures and then with their teacher's help to compose and transcribe accompanying texts. Widely reported elsewhere (see, for example, King, 1978, p. 29), the approach was of course not peculiar to this classroom. A second stemmed from her professional studies, through which she had become familiar with the 'language experience' approach to early literacy teaching. Thirdly, she was then working to the National Curriculum English framework which was current at the time (see DES, 1990). This emphasized narrative structure, sentence construction and conventional orthography. Finally, she took from her mentors a solution to the problem of classroom management. In this drawing served a dual function. For the pupils and Sally together, it provided a focus for the negotiation of the required sentences. For Sally herself, the relative independence with which the children could cope with the drawing task freed her to attend to what were seen as the more pressing demands of their writing (Sally, 1993d). Her actions, shaped by these four factors, and the readiness of the children to fall in with them, made them into the realities of the classroom.

In her careful drawing of the grave and its occupant, in her presentation of this drawing to Sally, in her readiness to negotiate a sentence to accompany it in the required declarative form, to transcribe the sentence and then to retranscribe it in the light of the conventional model offered, and then to repeat the cycle of activity in relation to the 'ending' of her text, Claire was conforming in the first instance, and at one level of subjectivity, to Sally's classroom reality. At another level, however, the congruence of their worlds was less complete. This related to the areas of indeterminacy in the reality Sally had defined: the content and the fictiveness of the children's texts. With regard to the latter, many of the children constructed imaginary worlds built on the light-hearted themes of *James and the Jungle*. Claire's world of the graveyard, however, was different. Far from lighthearted, it dealt, not with a fictive world, but with personal experience directly. Drawing on Dyson's scheme, one might suggest that, in making her drawing of the grave, she was moving 'inside a reflected world, (as) a reflective storyteller reliving past experiences' which were particular to her individual circumstances beyond school. How deeply this remembered world concerned her one cannot say. Nevertheless, its potential emotional charge is striking. It does not look like a world of peripheral significance, or one entered or departed from lightly.

Yet she did leave it, and abruptly. Having shown her initial drawing to Sally, she switched, firstly to the negotiation of a verbal statement, and then to its transcription, followed, as already indicated, by the colouring of the grave and the subsequent construction of a further drawing leading to the sentence, 'But my daddy's still alive'. In view of what it might mean for a 'reflective storyteller', and especially one so young, to move 'inside a remembered world' relating to the death and burial of a grandparent, the shifts from the apparent concern of the initial drawing to the colouring and then to the final text are remarkable. They look like disruptions of her movement in remembered realities, or, more precisely, the curtailment of their exploration and its diversion into particular channels, a disruption in two stages, the first involving the colouring and the second the formulation of the 'happy ending'.

This interpretation must be viewed cautiously. The act of colouring might have been cathartic, enabling Claire to put sombre thoughts behind her. In her final page, Claire might be seen as a story-teller acknowledging her reconciliation to a world of loss through a recognition of what remained. Nevertheless, there are grounds for accepting the disruption hypothesis. They relate to two things which especially invite explanation. One is Claire's colouring of the grave, an act which appears incongruous in the context of the remembered world of an internment. The second is the shift from this sombre focus to the formulation of a 'happy ending'.

The notion of disruption is supported firstly by Claire's observation about her colouring: 'My teacher likes us to colour things in bright colours'. The reality of the grave, one might suggest, was overtaken by the everyday, situated reality of the classroom, in which drawings were to be brightly coloured as a sequel to the completion of the writing tasks. Sally's own comments support the hypothesis of the subsequent diversion of Claire's movements into particular channels. She thought that she had not directly called for a happy ending. She believed, however, that in her pronouncements to the group as a whole she had emphasized conclusions of this kind. *James and the Jungle*, the book used to demonstrate what she was seeking, had ended in such vein. She had drawn attention to it. Moreover, most of the stories that the children met in their classroom, she believed, ended in that way (Sally, 1993d).

Up to a point, Claire was able through her drawing to determine the content of her texts. Between Sally and her there was scope for the negotiation of the sentences for transcription. However, it was Sally, adopting the practices of her mentors, who ensured, even if not consciously, the written statements' declarative form. It was Sally who effectively determined that Claire's written sentences should form the core of what was to be seen as a narrative with a beginning, middle and end to be 'published' in the form of a book. Most importantly, it was arguably Sally, and perhaps to a greater extent those to whose models of teaching she was according, who ensured that Claire's texts would reach a particular kind of conclusion.

One might conclude this stage by recognizing that, even though Claire could find within school some scope for exploring her realities beyond it, it was primarily Sally who determined the extent and mode by which they could be jointly considered. The incongruence between their respective worlds was largely masked by the realities defined through classroom practice. Claire, of course, inhabited both. The difference between them, however, lay in their provenance. The one stemmed from her own world of family; the other from a world of school. To inhabit the school world, as it was there defined, and what was entailed by being a pupil within it, was to curtail movement within other realities beyond it.

Narrative Awareness and Action in the Interests of Children

It is not difficult to find grounds for diverting children's attention from their worlds beyond school. In Claire's case, accession to the classroom reality could have contributed to her growing control, at a variety of levels, over the conventions of narrative writing. Consistent with an 'adult needs' view of English, interpreted in the Cox Report as calling, amongst other things, for an ability 'to write clearly, appropriately and effectively' (DES, 1988, para. 3.22), the acquisition of such control might indeed be held to be in her long-term interests, especially where writing's communicative role is emphasized.

An 'adult needs' conception, however, does not encompass all the purposes English might serve, nor does communication exhaust all of language's roles. Other possibilities for English noted by Cox include 'personal growth', which 'emphasises the relationship between language and learning in the individual child' (para. 3.20), and 'cultural analysis', highlighting 'the role of English in helping children towards a critical understanding of the world and cultural environment in which they live' (para. 3.24). Each of these embraces purposes for education generally. Each can be seen to be relevant to Claire's exploration of her paramount reality.

Of further functions claimed for language, not the least are heuristic and imaginative, and operate on an intra- as well as an interpersonal plane (see Halliday, 1969). Many would give weight to the particular title of writing as an instrument for thinking (see, for example, Smith, 1983). And narrative, conceived as a primary act of mind (Hardy, 1968), has long been held to play a central role in making experience meaningful. Story writing combines all these sense-making possibilities. With their life-long need to give meaning to experience in mind, the acquisition of a facility in written narrative may be seen to be much in pupils' interest.

For children, however, just as for adults, making sense of experience is not only for the morrow, but also a task in which they are daily engaged. Depicted by one writer as

> ... a ceaseless struggle with meaning, a prolonged effort of mind to shape and reshape experience in the face of new evidence, fresh concerns and developing ideas ... (Armstrong, 1990, p. 19)

it is a task to which the heuristic and imaginative functions of language generally, and narrative in particular, have immediate relevance. Where education is seen to be concerned with children as children as well as with future adult-hood, a conception to which both personal growth and cultural analysis views are pertinent, acting in children's interests will begin with and constantly re-turn to their struggle with meaning in the here and now. What is at issue at this point is what knowledge about narrative is relevant to the task and who should have it.

With regard to narrative as an act of mind and its linking to educational processes, two facets of such knowledge are of interest here. One relates to Dyson's studies, noted above, of novice writers. The multiple ways in which narrative can be mediated need to be appreciated. The other relates to what narrative structure does. In a passage germane to Claire's predicament, one writer claims that it facilitates of the invention of meaning:

> The unremitting flow of events must first be selectively attended to, interpreted as holding relationships, causes, motives, feelings, conse-quences — in a word, *meanings.* To give an order to this otherwise unmanageable flux we must . . . invent, yes, invent, beginnings and ends for out there are no such things. Even so stark an ending as death is only an ending when we have made a story out of life. This is the axiomatic element of narrative: it is the outcome of a mental process which enables us to excise from our experience a meaningful sequence, to place it within boundaries . . . to make it resonate in the contrived silences which may precede it and end it. (Rosen, 1985, p. 13, original emphasis)

There is no necessary connection, however, between explicit knowledge and what people can actually do. Where the construction of meaning — or the exploration of realities — is the goal, nothing said so far implies that children require explicit knowledge of narrative structure. From their social experience beyond school, however, they already have an implicit awareness of story as a meaning making resource. With both their current development and their future needs in mind, what is in their interests is its extension to embrace the possibilities of writing and its continued application to their quest for meaning. To these ends, explicit structural knowledge may be less significant than help in making their current experience resonant.

For adults, however, the implications are different. The personal growth and the cultural analysis arguments require them to work dialogically with the grain of children's concerns. To engage with children's understandings of their paramount reality, to assist in their review and transformation, it is the teachers who require explicit knowledge of how narrative works. Moreover, since they must both attend to the children's developing meanings and make contribu-tions from their own wider understandings in forms with which the children can connect, they must understand both its intramental and its intermental workings. They need to see narrative structure as a cultural resource for mediating the 'otherwise unimaginable flux' of experience through dialogue (inner and outer), rather than as an end in itself. Its relevance to the children's interests in this context is thus pedagogical rather than curricular, an aspect of explicit knowledge needed by teachers for deployment in the interests of children's meaning making.

The Ideology of an Opportunity Missed

What is interesting about Claire's book-making experience is not her entry into the world of the graveyard so much as her peremptory emergence from it. There was no shared exploration of what her grandfather had meant to her, no discussion of her feelings about his death, no consideration of what the burial rites meant to her and to others. Similarly, there were no contributions to Claire's concerns from the teacher's own experience or wider resources. The above analysis has suggested that the curtailment of Claire's exploration of her paramount reality reflected, not her autonomous movements within her inner world or the outer realities of her culture, so much as an accommodation to a classroom reality. Bearing in mind what more extended and shared explorations might have contributed to her personal growth and to her awareness of her culture, this looks like an opportunity for an educative encounter missed.

A consideration of the episode's typicality is beyond this chapter's scope. What is within its reach, however, is an exploration of the issues to which it gives rise should such incidents be common, and it is to this that I shall now turn. In particular, I want to consider the factors which appear to be associated with the curtailment of Claire's exploration of her world beyond school. I shall suggest that four in particular were involved and that, where ideology is seen in the terms proposed by Sharp and Green (see above), each is at root ideological.

The least obvious relates to the problem of class management. The press of classroom events on teachers is widely acknowledged (see Doyle, 1986, p. 394). Their need to find activities which do not call for supervision is real. Like many early years teachers, Sally saw drawing and colouring as activities which her pupils could cope with independently. There is nothing intrinsic to drawing or colouring, however, which frees them from the requirement of teacher attention. It is rather that they are conventionally thus constructed in teachers' realities. The consequence of this understandable management ploy, but less readily acknowledged ideological stance, may well be profound. Drawing and colouring, activities through which children may powerfully explore their re-membered realities, although widely practised, are effectively denied as locations for classroom dialogue. Their potential contribution to children's meaning making takes second place to other claims.

The reduction of the significance of children's drawing and colouring is further accentuated by the role these activities are seen to play in the processes of composition. Where text is regarded primarily as verbal and the goal is the articulation of a sentence that can be written down, what precedes the identification of an agreed statement assumes merely instrumental significance. Drawing's meaning-shaping potential is denied. The inner monologuing and interaction with others which commonly accompany it are unexploited. An activity inherently saturated in language is unrecognized as an arena for joint discourse. All that the teacher could contribute to the expressive reordering of the child's reality from her own experience or awareness of relevant literature and other cultural artefacts or practices is denied.

The constraints placed on children's exploration of their realities by the limited roles allocated to drawing and colouring are then buttressed by the 'morning assembly genre' of the sentences to which they lead. According to Christie,

> . . . the patterns of reasoning encoded in (such sentences) involve nothing of the speculation or enquiry which are ostensibly part of the purpose of education. (p. 245)

The genre underestimates children's intellectual powers. Its declarative statements contribute little to the reordering of their reality.

The account offered above, however, suggests that the intellectual expectations of Claire's classroom did not merely curtail the exploration of her reality. They also pushed her into the search for a 'happy ending'. Sally believed that she had not consciously steered things in this direction. At the same time, she was aware of the possible influence of the classroom's general bookstock and the particular work she had used. Her account matches an ideology of childhood innocence seen elsewhere in infant teaching:

> The state of innocence was not only recognized in the the teachers' interpretations of children's behaviour but also in the way in which they protected children from harmful and unpleasant aspects of the outside world . . . (King, 1978, p. 13)

That protectiveness was typically shown, King claimed, in relation to managing the knowledge of death. In this light, Claire's final statement, 'But my daddy's still alive', may owe as much to constructions of the world offered in the classroom as to any reformulation from within of her realities beyond it.

The final impediment to Claire's more extensive exploration of her beyond-school realities is provided by story structure being seen as a goal in itself. It should be clear from what has been said above that I do not wish to suggest that beginnings, middles and endings are without importance. The point that I want to make here is that prioritizing the construction of a narrative in the form of three written declaratives obscures the possibility that each sentence was but the tip of a significant narrative in its own right. In consequence, engagements with children's movements in remembered realities are minimalized. Excisions from the flux of experience, the identification of significant beginnings, middles and ends, are largely teacher-determined.

Concerns Arising

This account stems from the puzzlement of two practitioners about events encountered in the course of professional activity in which each was directly, but differently, involved. The nature of this activity meant that much data needed for their interpretation is missing. In consequence, any conclusions must be drawn with caution. Nevertheless, enough material is available to make speculation about general issues worthwhile.

It appears from this account that, in one context of literacy teaching, powerful factors conspired to constrain a novitiate teacher's engagement with a young child's beyond-school realities. In particular, they appear to have allowed only a superficial joint exploration of bereavement, a matter that might be seen to be of some importance to a child's developing awareness of herself and her world. These factors related to teacher action, by commission and omission, constrained by problems of class management and informed by understandings and beliefs about what it was appropriate to do in particular circumstances. Such understandings and beliefs, it has been suggested, are at root ideological.

These conjectures have been raised in a consideration of the work of a teacher at the threshold of professional life. It should be made clear that nothing said here is intended as a criticism of her work: no praise could be too high for her endeavours to take on the teaching role as it had been presented to her in precept and example. But here lies the rub, for underlying all that has been said is the sense of an educative opportunity missed. And it was missed, not for lack of diligence, but because a young person's professional lights precluded her from engaging other than superficially with a child's realities beyond school.

What needs to be considered here is what might be done to make the seizure of opportunities like this more likely, not just by Sally, but by teachers at large. The admittedly tentative speculations to which this brief episode have led suggest that the barriers lie not so much in teachers as individuals as in their shared professional realities. Of those which appear to bear directly on the episode described above and, by extension, on others like it, some are concrete and, in the present climate, scarcely open to change. Reductions in class size on a scale large enough to make class management significantly easier, for example, are unlikely to occur. Others, more obviously ideological, such as the conception of childhood innocence, may be so ingrained in the culture of early years education as to be resistant to short-term amendment.

Yet others, however, are more open to amendment, in that they are consciously shaped by human intellect and, within reasonable financial bounds, amenable to political decision. Among these are the intellectual tools and curriculum conceptions which inform teachers' daily work and the assessment context in which they are applied. One study (Desforges and Cockburn, 1987) has argued that getting these right is crucial to the improvement of mathematics education. Their comments might be applied with equal force to the field of early literacy, for some time now, within the National Curriculum, the province of 'English'.

The curriculum conceptions and assessment framework for writing available through the National Curriculum English at the time of Sally's work with Claire were markedly inhospitable to children's exploration, by any means available to them, of their beyond-school realities. They made but one mention of a link between pictures and writing. In requiring pupils to 'produce, independently, pieces of writing using complete sentences, some of them demarcated with capital letters and fullstops or question marks' (DES, 1990, AT3, Level 2), they did nothing to invite movement beyond the 'morning news genre' arguably so limiting to speculation and reasoning. In calling for children to be able to write stories 'showing the rudiments of story structure by establishing an opening, characters and one or more events' (Level 2), leading to 'more complex stories . . . with a defined ending' (Level 3), they emphasized narrative form as an end in itself, rather than for the heuristic purposes it might serve.

At first sight, the Dearing revisions might be taken to be favourable to a change of emphasis. For Key Stage 1, they indicate that pupils 'should be helped to understand the value of writing as a means of remembering, communicating, organising and developing ideas . . .' (SCAA, 1994, p. 9). But, while explicit reference to 'beginnings, middles and ends' is dropped, the overwhelming emphasis is on the structural features, varieties of form and presentational skills which contribute to communicative competence. Of the conjunction of writing and drawing, which might have been presented as a multi-media device which may be employed in the construction of meaning, there is no sign whatsoever. Instead, what is accentuated is a trend apparent in the earlier framework. It construes children as producers, there to shape artifacts for other people's consumption, an instrumentalist conception well-suited to consumerist times and to the belief that the main concern of human interaction is with the efficient passage of information between one person and another.

What is absent from all this is any recognition of the significance of Hardy's famed claim that:

> . . . we dream in narrative, daydream in narrative, remember, anticipate, hope, despair, believe, doubt, plan, revise, criticize, construct, gossip, learn, hate, and love by narrative. (Hardy, 1968, p. 13)

The point here is that young children already know something of the power of narrative from their world beyond school, are well able to use language for more than declarative purposes (see, for example, Wells, 1986), and can employ drawing powerfully to explore both actual and possible worlds. What school offers as an introduction to literacy, one might suggest, could well embrace what children know and can do, but in a deeper sense of 'knowing' and 'doing' than is expressed in much of the current rhetoric of education, and support them in their use of these facilities in the endeavour to determine who they are, what this world is that we live in and how we live together within it. Such an approach would regard narrative, not as an end in itself, but as a cultural practice, available to the individual, or, for that matter, the group, as a device for the contemplation and transformation of both inner and outer reality, of individual and social life.

To see narrative in this way is to allow the educator to work with the grain of children's 'ceaseless struggle with meaning' and to recognize that this begins with and constantly returns to their everyday reality. It is also to acknowledge that the shaping and reshaping of experience is undertaken by the exchange of ideas well as by individual effort and that the cumulative meanings of society and the ways in which they are symbolized are resources on which individuals can draw, contribute to and even change. In this context, it is especially to see that children can be supported in their struggle through the narratives of their culture, and that some of the richest are created and offered through multi-media activity. John Burningham's *Granpa*, for example, might have something to say to children like Claire, whose everyday reality gives her her own reasons for thinking about beginnings, middles and ends. The problem for the teacher is to recognize and embrace them, and, for those who shape teachers' realities, to make make it all possible. In both its early form and its latest manifestation, National Curriculum English, does not help.

References

ARMSTRONG, M. (1990) 'Does the National Curriculum rest on a mistake?' in EVERTON, P., MAYNE, P. and WHITE, S. (Eds) *Effective Learning: Into a New ERA*, London, Jessica King Publishers.

BERGER, P. and LUCKMAN, T. (1966) *The Social Construction of Reality*, Harmondsworth, Penguin Books.

CHRISTIE, F. (1987) 'Young children's writing: From spoken to written genre' in CARTER, R. (Ed) *Knowledge About Language*, London, Hodder and Stoughton.

DES (1988) *English for Ages 5 to 11* (The Cox Report), London, HMSO.

DES (1990) *English in the National Curriculum (No. 2)*, London, HMSO.

DESFORGES, C. and COCKBURN, A. (1987) *Understanding the Mathematics Teacher*, London, Falmer Press.

DOYLE, W. (1986) 'Classroom organization and management' in WITTROCK, M.C. (Ed) *Handbook of Research on Teaching* (3rd edn), New York, Macmillan.

DYSON, A.H. (1988) 'Negotiating among multiple worlds: The space/time dimensions of young children's composing', *Research in the Teaching of English*, **22**, 4, December.

HALLIDAY, M.A.K. (1969) 'Relevant models of language', *Educational Review*, **22**, 1.

HARDY, B. (1968) 'Towards a poetics of fiction: an approach through narrative' reprinted in MEEK, M. *et al.* (1977) *The Cool Web*, London, Bodley Head.

KING, R.A. (1978) *All Things Bright and Beautiful?*, Chichester, John Wiley and Sons.

MARTIN, J.R. and ROTHERY, J. (1980 and 1981) Writing Project Reports, Nos. 1 and 2, *Working Papers in Linguistics*, Sydney, Linguistics Department, University of Sydney.

Rosen, H. (1985) *Stories and Meanings*, Sheffield, National Association for the Teaching of English.

Sally (1993a) lesson plans, *Teaching Practice File*.

Sally (1993b) lesson evaluation, *Teaching Practice File*.

Sally (1993c) letter to author.

Sally (1993d) conversation with author.

SCAA (1994) *English in the National Curriculum: Draft Proposals*, London, Crown.

Sharp, R. and Green, A. (1975) *Education and Social Control*, London, Routledge and Kegan Paul.

Smith, F. (1983) 'A metaphor for literacy — Creating worlds or shunting information?' in Smith, F. (1983) *Essays into Literacy*, Portsmouth, NH, Heinemann, pp. 117–34.

Wells, G. (1986) *The Meaning Makers*, London, Hodder and Stoughton.

4   Controlling the Wild Things: A Critical Consideration of National Curriculum Documentation for Reading at Key Stages 1 and 2

Elizabeth Wilton Housego

In recent weeks I have been spending time with a group of 7 and 8-year-old pupils, reading with them Maurice Sendak's well-known picture book *Where The Wild Things Are* (1980). Max, the child hero, is rude to his mother, calling her a 'wild thing' and is sent to his room without his supper. Soon, a forest begins to grow in the room and Max sails to a far away land inhabited by strange monsters, the Wild Things. Although only small, Max tames them by staring into their eyes without blinking once and becomes their king, presiding over a celebratory wild rumpus. Eventually he decides that he wants to be where someone 'loved him best of all' and, returning home, finds supper waiting for him in his bedroom 'and it was still hot'.

The text functions at different levels and, using the wild things as metaphors for powerful emotion, it seems to me to give children opportunities to explore their own strong inner emotions and to consider power relationships in the wider world. As I talked with the pupils individually and listened intently to how they reacted to the story, I began to consider how our interactions fitted in to successive official documentation about responses to literature and in particular to the post-Dearing revised version. I, too, began to consider power relationships within the wider world and ask what constraints and opportunities the post-Dearing document offers to those of us who enjoy sharing literature with children. I began to realize that successive outpourings of official documentation and the political machinations which have surrounded the rewrites, have stirred within me feelings of extreme disquiet and raised in my mind a number of significant issues.

In considering these matters I have chosen to adopt a narrow focus and consider in detail some aspects of reading and literature study at Key Stages 1 and 2. It seems to me, however, that many of the points I am making apply to other aspects of English and perhaps even more generally across the primary curriculum. In the forthcoming pages, I shall draw attention to the increasing Government interference in relevant official documentation for reading and literature study in the primary school, with particular reference to the 1995

Orders. I shall identify the assumptions and different positions which seem to underpin the changing official words. I shall suggest that the present official position in relation to reading literature lies uneasily beside much recent thinking in the academic world. It is, I believe, not based on new theoretical understandings nor on careful research findings. Neither does it originate in thoughtful professional discourse amongst those who spend their lives teaching young people. Rather, it is largely rooted in the assertions of professional politicians and the official bodies appointed by them who, for the most part, seem to have little understanding either of how children learn or of recent thinking in the field of reading and response to literature. What they do have is considerable expertise in the manipulation of power and the ability to make confident public assertions. Yet, and this point needs to be considered with grave concern, it is these people who have taken it upon themselves to redefine the very nature of what reading involves and hence how professionals should go about their work in classrooms.

Government dissatisfaction with the original National Curriculum English document is now a familiar story and few were surprised when a review was ordered. Those who studied the 1993 redraft became aware of significant changes. In all aspects of language, what Dombey (1993) termed the 'strident' voices of the political right were clear for all to see. In reading there was a strong emphasis on the teaching and practising of skills, on phonics and adherence to conventions; accurate decoding was the main goal for young readers. Dombey also identified the presence of some 'gentler voices' which, echoing the thinking in the Cox Report, prioritized both meaning and children's perspectives. These gentler voices paid greater respect to children and implicitly made a plea for more sensitive and courteous interactions with young learners.

The slimmed down 1995 post-Dearing documentation gives similar evidence of the 'strident' and 'gentler' voices coming together in an uneasy synthesis. The strident voices are again dominant at Key Stages 1 and 2, underpinned by unexamined assumptions and a brisk, no nonsense approach which begs many questions and carries serious implications for the health of a democratic society. The gentler and more subtle voices are not altogether absent but are being shouted down. The pages which follow represent a plea that we, like the technicians in a recording studio, amplify the volume of the gentler voices and listen to the wisdom they contain.

In analyzing the reading/literature aspects of the 1995 post-Dearing document, it is important to look for perceived positive, as well as negative, features and these will, of course, depend upon the individual's particular philosophical perspective. For me and for many teachers, it is encouraging to see emphasis on children coming into contact with a broad range of texts, including those on computer screens. No child's experience of reading will be limited and shaped by reading schemes alone and this is further ensured by the type of literary texts required to be used for SATS at Key Stage 1. It is also encouraging to see emphasis on children being encouraged to develop and use a range of reading strategies, depending on their purpose for reading. This satisfaction, however, is marred by a number of significant and profoundly disquieting features within the literature aspect of the documentation, features which need to be examined in some detail.

Subjugation of Children's Voices

The first major criticism is concerned with the subjugation of children's voices. Instead of emphasizing children's quest for meaning, it emphasizes a skills approach, drawing attention to what Smith (1985) has termed 'the window pane' and not 'the view beyond'. Here I need to clarify my own position. I am not against the careful and explicit teaching of skills: indeed I believe this to be essential to the empowerment of readers. What needs to come first, however, and what gives point to the learning of skills, is the need to engage with meaning. When sharing *Where The Wild Things Are* (Sendak, 1980) with the children, I was interested to pick up their many and varied concerns and to see how they related their worlds to that of Sendak's text. One child in the group, Theo, has a profoundly handicapped sister and is well aware of the love and sacrifices needed from all the family in caring for her in her own home. Many of the family routines have had to be constructed around the needs of the little girl and the family members not only enjoy and learn from her but also have to make sacrifices. Theo felt able to express his own agenda as he showed a concern with family love. Why, he wondered, was Max content to return to a place where just one person loved him best of all. 'All my family love me!' he confided. As Theo has gained more experience of the wider world and the ways other families live their lives, he is probably aware that his family is special and that there are particular bonds and responsibilities which both enrich and challenge his family members. He probably has a richer view of family interdependence than many other members of his class and is seeking to refine his understanding of his own and other people's families. He also enquired, 'How did Max know that they (the Wild Things) didn't love him much?' Could love in other families be more conditional, more limited, than in his own and how might this be evidenced? Here, I would suggest, Theo is still looking at group dynamics of living together in communities and wondering how discord or coolness of feeling might be shown. Most teachers of young children would agree that home life is the most important factor in their pupils' lives and it is the refinement of thinking on this highly significant matter which constituted Theo's agenda.

If children are to learn that reading is a worthwhile activity which has something to offer to them and hence is worth the considerable effort involved in becoming a reader, then their interests, meanings and concerns need to be acknowledged, engaged with and honoured. I am not suggesting here that teachers have no agendas of their own. Clearly they do. As Donaldson (1986) has also shown, however, the artistry of teaching lies in managing the subtle interplay of agendas between learner and teacher throughout the curriculum.

Elizabeth Wilton Housego

Children need to learn that there is an interplay between the world they create with the text, the world where they lead their lives and their own inner lives. Without this interplay, she claims, there is little point to reading.

An Authority Dependent View of Meaning in Texts

Secondly, the meanings which children will create when reading are subjugated to the underpinning assumption that there is one meaning to be gleaned from reading a text and that this is identified by the person in authority. This reverts to much earlier notions held by proponents of the New Criticism Movement in the earlier part of this century and associated particularly with the names of I.A. Richards and F.R. Leavis. Evidence that such thinking underpins the official view of reading is seen as we read in the Programmes of Study that: 'In understanding and responding to stories and poems, pupils should be given opportunities to explain the content of a passage or whole text' (POS for Reading, para. 2c). From a New Criticism perspective, texts were cultural artefacts whose true meaning would only be found if readers were able to divest themselves of personal qualities, personality traits, background and past experiences and approach the text in an objective way . . . to read, in fact, in the role of detached critic. The central question to be asked was, 'Is it in the text?' and students would be driven back to seek textual evidence for viewpoints. This close scanning of texts for evidence is clearly evident in the 1995 post-Dearing National Curriculum documentation as in the following: 'pupils should be taught . . . to refer to relevant passages or episodes to support their opinions' (P13 POS Key Skills, 2a). Since teachers would be likely to have a greater familiarity with texts being studied, so the power structures within lecture theatres and classrooms reflected this unequal status. Individuals were urged to look outside themselves, to subjugate personal response to the authority of the text itself and to that of well informed teachers who could lead them to 'correct' understanding.

It is not until much later in the document, within the implied model of reading development found in the level descriptions for reading, that there is any acknowledgement of the way children will make personal and idiosyncratic responses to texts. Here, as late as level 7, it is stated that pupils will 'articulate personal . . . responses to poems, plays and novels . . .' although even this statement is framed and controlled by officialdom, for the sentence continues, 'showing awareness of their thematic, structural and linguistic features'. This implicit assumption that, for young children at least, there is a single textual meaning which children in the earlier stages of reading should seek out, leaves no space for the varied meanings which were apparent when children studied Sendak's text with me. Reference has already been made to Theo's agenda but this was not shared by all the other pupils. Vicky, for example, was preoccupied with animals' claws and the purposes they serve,

66

Simon focused on changes in the physical environment and April spent considerable time thinking about security and safety issues.

The authority dependent view of reading is clearly evident in the post-Dearing documentation and ignores the thinking of Reader Response theorists. Although, as Benton (1992) has pointed out, Reader Response criticism is 'a very broad church' (p. 3), its theorists share certain principles, drawing attention away from the text itself and emphasizing the relationship of reader and text in acts of cocreation. Benton and Fox (1985) have pointed out that readers will picture, anticipate, retrospect, enact with and evaluate texts in idiosyncratic ways. The individuality of responses is achieved through the different life experiences, personality and purposes of the reader and is different for every reading, even re-readings of the same text.

This is not to say that teachers will encourage wild, indisciplined responses; indeed discipline is important. The chosen genre and words of the text offer limitations and constraints as well as opportunities, to the reader as to the author. There is a further need for discipline, too, as people of whatever age, share their individual responses, listening carefully to each other, comparing and contrasting their perceptions with those of others, and building up multi-faceted responses. All this, however, finds little echo or acknowledgement in the 1995 Programmes of Study for Key Stages 1 and 2. The meaning of literature, it implies, is clear for all to read and can be conveyed unproblematically to others rather than being continually constructed afresh in individual and collaborative engagements with text.

Some might protest that the documentation does make reference to meaning. True, mention is made to pupils understanding the different meanings of 'words and their use and interpretation in different contexts' (Key Stage 1, 3b) and there is instruction that attention should be given to relationships between root words and derivatives and prefixes and suffixes (Key Stage 1, 2b). Meaning, however, is associated with individual words rather than longer pieces of discourse and there is little evidence that the writers of the documentation appreciate the complexities of how children construct meaning as they read.

A Minimalist View of What Constitutes Reading

The 1995 documentation has another major flaw in that it presents a minimalist model of what constitutes reading. In the process of streamlining documentation, the view of what happens when children read has emerged as a poor, emaciated creature, one which ignores much of what we have come to know about the nature of reading and what it can do to and for people. The worry is that once this poor creature is enshrined in print, and in official documentation at that, it assumes a status and authority which it does not merit. What is not mentioned may be seen as unimportant. In what sense, then, is the new official view of reading to be seen as an emaciated creature? How does it underestimate what children are able to do when reading texts?

Little Concern for the Development of Children's Inner Lives

First, there is no apparent appreciation of the opportunities which literature offers for pupils' imaginative and emotional development. In recent years much has been written about the way stories allow children to recognize, reflect upon and come to terms with their own inner worlds. Chambers (1983) has shown how children can learn more about themselves and others as they imaginatively project themselves into alternative worlds which exist in other times and other places. The child psychiatrist and educator Bruno Bettelheim (1975) has shown the way in which stories can help children come to terms, at different levels of the mind, with such things as the transition from dependence to independence, growing sexuality, loss, sibling rivalry, the essential loneliness of the human condition and so on.

The strong emotional satisfaction felt by 8-year-old Avril was apparent as she reached the ending of Sendak's text. 'I like the bit,' she announced (quoting the book) 'when Max sails back over a year and in and out of weeks and through a day'. I just like it when he gets back and has his supper ready and took off his monster suit'. The rhythms of the language and the return to safe normality evoked in Avril a strong affective response upon which she could usefully reflect. Another child, Mark, pondered upon the ambivalent feelings which he had towards his own mother when she was cross with him. For children, this can be a frightening experience since the mother with whom they may feel angry is also the source of their security and well being. Literature can offer comfort by showing that others, too, feel such things. Moreover, some texts, as Bettelheim (1976) points out, allow children to express such ambivalence safely by allowing positive feelings to be projected on to the 'good' (often dead) parent and negative feelings on to a wicked stepmother. Concern with such responses, however, is absent and therefore, by implication, not valued in the official rhetoric. It is, to say the least, disquieting to see either ignorance of, or deliberate turning away from, theoretical perspectives which have recognized the power of literature to touch children's inner lives.

Little Concern with Conceptual Matters

Secondly, there is an arbitrary and minimal selection of statements about what children need to know about texts and reading. Cueing strategies and phonic skills are emphasized but there are huge and significant omissions, particularly in relation to conceptual understanding.

Meek (1988), for instance, has pointed to the important conceptual lessons about reading which children learn over time when engaging with picture books. Through the subtle interplay of written text and pictures by such author/illustrators as John Burningham, Anthony Browne and Janet and Allan Ahlberg, children can see complex literary devices illustrated in tangible form before their eyes. Meek suggests that these include the presence of simultaneous happenings, deliberate omission, irony, plots within plots, intertextuality, different perspectives held by different characters, that the reader may be 'in the know' when characters are not and much more. An adult who is attending with care to children is able to identify quite sophisticated understanding about such things, albeit expressed in simple words and with frequent use of children's hands to help them explain matters which may be above their oral competence. This sort of understanding about the nature of reading and texts which Meek has explicated with such care and expertise is again notable by its absence.

Little Concern with Active Evaluation of Texts

Another serious factor is the limited and low expectation of children who are generally perceived as passive receivers of texts. There is no reference to interrogative reading at Key Stage 1 and just one at Key Stage 2 when pupils should be taught to 'consider an argument critically' (2c p. 14). Why is the documentation content with critical thought just in relation to an argument? Why is interrogative reading not encouraged across a range of genres? Although at Key Stage 2 children are expected to 'pose pertinent questions' (POS, 2c, p. 14), this is only in relation to non-fiction which has been until recently a somewhat neglected area of the reading curriculum. Mallett (1994), however, has detailed many useful approaches to address pupils' difficulties in reading non fiction. Amongst these, and in order to minimize the copying of chunks of text as part of curriculum units, she has advocated that children generate their own questions prior to reading non fiction texts. Whilst it is is encouraging to see at least part of Mallett's thinking represented in the post-Dearing documentation, it is necessary to ask why such questioning of texts is limited to non-fiction and why, even then, it is disregarded until Key Stage 2. More importantly, the sort of questions which are implied in the documentation are of a particular type. They seek out factual information rather than being of a more critical order. Little credit is given to children, like Richard, who adopt a more interrogative approach towards texts. 'Why?' Richard asked, 'did the Wild Things tell Max that they would eat him up . . . because he was king?'. This little boy drew upon his knowledge of power relationships within his family and the natural world and knew that people and animals rarely threaten those more powerful than themselves. He was therefore able to articulate a perceived mismatch between what he knew and what he had just read in the text. Children were also able to articulate evaluative stances towards texts. Katie explained that she was glad that Max had been sent to bed without supper for being rude to his mother since that was 'the right thing for his mother to have done'. When Vicky read Sendak's text she was reminded of *Peter and the Wolf*, a text which also contained an untamed creature. She claimed that it contained a mistake because 'it was mean because the wolf tried to get the bird. I won't read that again. No way!' This comment, whilst at first seeming to indicate lack of conceptual understanding of what constitutes a mistake, may in fact give evidence of the adoption of a moral stance towards the subject matter by a child who finds it difficult to come to terms with the idea of food chains. Yet another sort of evaluative response to the text was evidenced by Simon who, at 8 years of age, showed that he was able to read the text from different perspectives and that this is not the sole prerogative of such undergraduate courses as feminist or Marxist approaches to literature. 'I'd have liked it if I were Max,' he explained, 'but I don't like it when I'm Simon because Max gets to do exciting things and I don't.'

It is important that such active and evaluative responses are valued and encouraged by teachers and parents. If we wait until children can read reasonably fluently and accurately before introducing them to ideas of readers interrogating and reflecting upon texts, it may well be too late. By then, they may well feel overwhelmed by the authority and status of the printed word. Disturbingly, they may have learnt that their voice does not count and that they have no right to question or offer comment . . . that this is not part of the reading process and that authority lies with others. Thus, as Belenky and Blyth *et al.* (1986) have shown in their study of American women, many people carry with them into life a passive, externally orientated perspective on knowledge and knowing which disempowers them.

The Narrow Focus of Level Descriptions

The impoverished view of what constitutes reading is clearly evidenced in the Level Descriptions of the post-Dearing documentation. Within these, recognition is given to easily identifiable achievements and performance whilst ignoring more sophisticated aspects of children's learning.

Vygotsky (1978) has drawn attention to the 'buds' of learning which with support will grow and develop; he pointed to what children are able to do in the company of a more experienced person but not yet manage alone. Such buds are not recognized within Level Descriptions even though they are significant to the child's learning. April, for instance, would be given no credit for reading Sendak's text alongside me when she lacked the confidence and some of the skills to read everything independently. The thinking of Vygotsky who emphasized the scaffolding of pupils' learning experiences, is thus effectively ignored.

Similarly, little attention is paid to what Piaget identified as children's schematas, their ways of looking at the world. Some of these may be in tune with conventional thinking in society but others are not and may need to be challenged, as I noted during my interactions with the pupils. During this time it became increasingly clear that the children were reading Sendak's text at a literal rather than allegorical level. They seemed to feel that any text which did not present the world in the exact way they experienced it was 'wrong'. Martin looked carefully at pictures which showed Max's room being transformed into a forest before asserting, 'The forest can't grow in a room so that's a mistake . . . you could call that a mistake.' Luke did not like the way Max's supper was described as 'still hot' even though he had been away for a long time sailing, 'in and out of weeks and almost over a year to where the wild things are'. His own experience led him to know that hot food soon goes cold so he announced that the story was a bit strange at this point, that he didn't really like it and that it was 'wrong'.

From these comments I learned a great deal about the children's developing schemata. Although they knew a great deal about stories and reading they had not yet understood that the willing suspension of disbelief which they employ so readily in play, may need to be engaged when reading some works of fiction. Importantly, they had not yet realized that there may be different levels of truth within texts and that Sendak is focussing upon the psychological rather that the literal so that it might be inappropriate to use literal matches with their own experience in order to challenge his text. They had also yet to understand the symbolic nature of either the wild things themselves or the hot supper which awaited Max on his return home. Over time, some of these existing schematas will need to be gently challenged and the children will need to be introduced to models of critical discourse by those more experienced than themselves so that they can develop as critical readers. Sadly the insights of Vygotsky and Piaget find no echo either in the Programmes of Study or the Level Descriptions, despite the centrality of these ideas to teaching and learning in primary classrooms.

Whose View Counts?

So far I have tried to show that the general thrust of the 1995 rewrite of National Curriculum English is towards a skills-based, competency-focused model which does not prioritize the making and negotiation of meaning, pays little attention to the voices of primary aged children and presents a seriously limited view of both reading and learning. Instead, efficient conformity seems to be valued, at least until children have reached a certain level of competence. The children we teach are to be tamed, rather like the Wild Things, into safe conformity. Surely they and society deserve more?

Meek (1992/93), writing about the 1993 new Orders which similarly sought to control and subject children in the various aspects of the language curriculum, made precisely this point. She ended her article on a boldly subversive note stressing that, 'we cannot go back on what we know now about children learning to read and write and using talk to learn, which is why, despite all the attempts to reconstitute literacy in terms of correct, constrained behaviour, limited entitlement, policed speech, we shall, before long, find ways of breaking free' (p. 32). Meek's point about 'going back', offering less than the best we know, goes to heart of the matter. As professional educators the important questions which we have to address with courage are, 'Whose judgments of quality count in the primary curriculum?' and, 'Are our judgments worth fighting for?'

References

BELENKY, M.F. and BLYTH, M.C. *et al.* (1986) *Women's Ways of Knowing: The Development of Self, Voice and Mind*, Basic Books, Inc.

BENTON, M. (1992) *Secondary Worlds*, Milton Keynes, Open University Press.

BENTON, M. and Fox, G. (1985) *Teaching literature 9–13*, Oxford, Oxford University Press.

BETTELHEIM, B. (1976) *The Uses of Enchantment*, London, Thames and Hudson.

CHAMBERS, A. (1983 revised & expanded) *Introducing Books to Children*, London, Heinemann Educational.

DOMBEY, H. (1992/93) 'Some thoughts on the proposal for reading', *Language Matters*, **3**, CLPE.

DONALDSON, M. (1986) *Children's Minds*, London, Fontana.

MALLETT, M. (1994) *Reading Non-fiction in the Primary Years*, Sheffield, National Association for the Teaching of English.

MEEK SPENCER, M. (1988) *How Texts Teach What Readers Learn*, Stroud, Thimble Press.

MEEK SPENCER, M. (1992/93) 'Implied literacy', *Language Matters*, **3**, CLPE.

SENDAK, M. (reprinted 1980) *Where the Wild Things Are*, London, Picture Puffins.

SMITH, F. (1985) *Reading*, Cambridge, Cambridge University Press.

VYGOTSKY, L. (1978) *Mind in Society: The Development of Higher Psychological Procedures*, Cambridge, MA, Harvard University Press.

5 The Glue That Sticks: Quality Assurance and Art Coordination in the Primary School

Stephen Howarth and Chris Burns

In many respects, the 1990s have been crucial years for art coordinators. Like coordinators in other subject areas, they have emerged from a rather shadowy and ill-defined past to occupy a key role in determining policy and practice in primary schools, at least according to official rhetoric (Webb, 1994).

Three influences appear to have combined to raise their status within schools:

- the scale and pace of change demanded by the implementation of the Education Reform Act (ERA), in particular the introduction of the local management of schools (LMS) which triggered a significant shift in the work of headteachers and so, in turn, of other staff (DFE, 1993a);
- the exponential increase in subject knowledge, skills and understanding required to deliver the post-ERA curriculum effectively which, coupled with LMS, made it impossible for primary headteachers to retain their traditional curriculum management and development role. Necessarily, headteachers delegated many of these responsibilities to coordinators (Osborn and Black, 1994);
- the introduction of new, public inspection criteria by the Office for Standards in Education (OFSTED) which require that coordinators have clearly defined subject responsibilities and that their role in school management is identified, particularly in relation to quality assurance processes (OFSTED, 1994b and 1995b).

The potential importance of coordinators in implementing and facilitating curriculum reform has been recognized by central government through the provision of centrally-funded in-service courses designed to enhance subject knowledge and curriculum leadership skills. OFSTED has already linked the effective deployment of art coordinators with improved standards in teaching and learning (OFSTED, 1995a).

However, the next few years are far from certain. Coordination remains an ambiguous activity, hovering somewhere in the twilight between the headteacher's responsibility for whole-school management and the classroom authority of the teacher (Bush, 1993). Post-ERA, few schools appear to have come to a collective view of the parameters of their coordinators' work (Webb, 1994).

This chapter argues that OFSTED's expectation that art coordinators will play a key part in monitoring and evaluating the curriculum has provided the opportunity to locate the role more firmly and convincingly within the management structures of primary schools. At the same time, this emerging role in quality assurance may provide the glue by which each of the more familiar aspects of coordination — providing subject expertise, supporting staff development, managing resources, leading curriculum planning, advising on assessment and liaising with parents and governors — can be held together and made coherent.

Meeting this expectation will require a major reconceptualization of coordination by senior managers in primary schools. For their part, coordinators will have to extend their expertise and develop new skills in assessing pupils' work, in planning, monitoring and evaluation. In addition, art coordinators are likely to have their own particular set of challenges related to subject status, their general lack of institutional seniority and the timing of the introduction of the Orders.

The Art Coordinator's Current Context

The context for coordinating art in primary schools is reasonably promising, in so far as the Statutory Order for Art appears to have been accepted positively. An extensive survey by Clement indicated that the majority of headteachers and teachers welcomed the Order. It was seen to provide, amongst other things, a 'framework for planning and progression' and to 'raise the profile of the subject in primary schools' (Clement, 1994, p. 18). Teachers were aware of, and generally accepted, the challenges to their own expertise offered by the Order, in particular by attainment target 2, which requires that children study the work of other artists as well as making their own. They recognized, too, the need to develop new and appropriate means of monitoring children's progress and assessing their achievements. According to Clement, art coordinators generally felt themselves to be more confident than their colleagues in their readiness to deliver the Order successfully. However, more than a third of them felt in need of some help and a little more than half considered themselves to be suitably experienced to meet some aspects, but not all, of the statutory requirements (Clement, 1993).

The recent OFSTED review of inspection findings relating to art at Key Stages 1 and 2 confirms a relatively satisfactory position and supports the optimism found by Clement (OFSTED, 1995a). Pupils are reported to be enthusiastic about art. Their work is 'lively and expressive' (p. 3). Standards of achievement in relation to their abilities are 'satisfactory or better' in some 70 per cent of lessons (*ibid.*). This compares favourably with the situation before the introduction of the Order, when HMI reported that art work in the majority of primary classes visited was adequate, but poor in about a third (DES, 1990).

However, some aspects of provision continue to give cause for concern. Standards are limited by a combination of low expectations of pupils and lack of teacher confidence in encouraging pupils to critically evaluate their own work. Three dimensional work is still uncommon. Skills, knowledge and understanding are rarely developed systematically. Work relating to famous artists too often results in pupils simply copying paintings with little reference to their spiritual, moral, cultural or social contexts. Much is still to be done in developing whole-school guidelines and schemes of work. Little progress has been made in assessing, recording and reporting (OFSTED, 1995a). Art coordinators have produced policies, but 'having little or no non-contact time, their influence on planning, monitoring and evaluating the art curriculum is minimal' (p. 4).

OFSTED's findings raise important questions about the subject expertise required if art coordinators are to monitor, evaluate and develop the practice of their colleagues, their capacity to affect change and the relationship of their work to school management as a whole. These issues are considered below.

Subject Expertise

The introduction of the Order and the inspection criteria for primary schools, taken together, have meant that several different kinds of expertise are now required of art coordinators. They are expected to have *pedagogical* expertise. They need to know about the subject in action in the classroom, appropriate teaching strategies, the most effective means to promote children's learning, how to exploit the use of information technology and language opportunites in art and how to recognize and plan for progression in the art curriculum. Importantly, they will require a sound knowledge of children's development in art in order to evaluate learning and assess standards of achievement.

Art coordinators need to understand the fourfold nature of the *aesthetic process* and its central concepts of 'making, presenting, responding and evaluating' (Taylor and Andrews, 1993, p. 15). This model provides a holistic and cohesive framework both for planning children's experiences in art and for extending children's personal thinking. It can draw together attainment target 1 and attainment target 2, connecting children's own work with art made by others, 'across time and place' (*ibid.*, p. 18). Without this framework, the relationship between the two may be difficult to make, a concern expressed by OFSTED inspectors.

They need to know about statutory requirements and feel secure in their own *subject knowledge*. But, in addition, their role in curriculum planning, particularly at the whole-school level, requires an understanding of the deeper *epistemological* assumptions underpinning the national curriculum and its division into separate subject areas (Kelly, 1995). Questions about the nature of art and its treatment within the primary curriculum — a subject to be taught through others or a subject to be taught in its own right — are fundamental to thinking about the art curriculum and have been so for some time (Piotrowski, 1995). At the moment, art still seems to be used primarily to support topic work (Budge, 1995).

It is difficult to justify the subject-based structure of the National Curriculum for primary schools or argue that its treatment of the arts demonstrates any particular understanding of them as 'a single community within the curriculum' (Abbs, 1987, p. 3). Art and music are defined as separate subjects, dance included within physical education, drama within English and media studies is apparently everywhere and nowhere. These divisions are founded on a rationalist epistemology which seeks to justify the separation of knowledge into disciplines — often translated into curriculum subjects — by analysis of their modes of enquiry and the particular questions that they ask about everyday experiences (Kelly, 1995). Whatever the arguments about the legitimacy of subjects or where boundaries may or may not be drawn, they do provide a means of thinking about and planning the curriculum. Subject disciplines make up the statutory framework within which art coordinators have to operate. To work confidently within this framework, they need an understanding of the nature of their subject, its central concepts, its paradigms and modes of enquiry. In art, this enquiry will include art criticism (Aubrey, 1994b).

The same rationalist epistemology also underpins the guidance on curriculum planning offered to primary schools by the National Curriculum Council (1993) and the School Curriculum Assessment Authority (1995) and is embedded in the criteria for the inspection of schools (OFSTED, 1994b and 1995b). The SCAA guidance suggests that schools identify:

- blocked units — distinct aspects of the subject which can exist as discrete and cohesive units of work;
- continuing work — those aspects of the subject which require regular ongoing teaching and assessment;
- linked units — those aspects of the subject which can be drawn together with other subjects to provide a coherent learning experience, where learning in one area supports and complements that in another.

If these allocations are to be more than arbitrary, coordinators must have an appropriate conceptual framework, based on a clear epistemological understanding of the unique contribution of art to the primary curriculum, to inform their planning.

There is a further kind of 'subject' expertise now required of coordinators by the OFSTED inspection criteria; that related to the *subject's potential contribution to the spiritual, moral, social and cultural development* of pupils within the school. The art coordinator is expected to ensure that planned opportunities for engagement with these issues occur in the art curriculum. Such opportunities may be found, for example, in discussion of the themes and significance of works of art and in teaching and learning experiences which enhance the pupil's capacity to respond to personal and social issues, to make judgments, to take risks and to work collaboratively. Our work with art coordinators indicates that this is an aspect of their work with which they are least familiar. Indeed, many are surprised to find this area included within their subject management responsibilities at all.

A Role in Search of a Position?

The introduction of the ERA has been mirrored by an increase in the number of art coordinators; a function of increasing delegation of subject leadership by headteachers in the wake of LMS and the introduction of new conditions of service which enabled curriculum management responsibilities to be placed on all teachers (DES, 1987). The HMI Primary Survey of 1978 indicated that some 31 per cent of surveyed schools had a teacher with special responsibility for art (DES, 1978). By 1992 Clement's survey of 570 primary schools in England and Wales was indicating that 82 per cent (467 schools) had a coordinator for art (Clement, 1993). OFSTED's review of findings from inspections during 1993/94 indicated that most, but not all, of its sample of seventy-nine primary schools had coordinators for art. These figures indicate a marked trend towards increased delegation of responsibilities for art. However, the staffs of primary schools are typically too small to allow one teacher to be matched with responsibilities for just one subject. Therefore, art subject responsibilities are often combined with those for other areas of the curriculum. Generally, coordinators in primary schools on average each carry responsibilities for between 1.5 and 2.2 subjects depending upon school size (Campbell and Neill, 1994).

The process of delegating curriculum leadership tended to follow the introduction of the Programmes of Study. As art, PE and music were the last three orders to come on stream, 'unless coordinating these subjects was already the responsibility of members of staff, there was no one left to whom further responsibilities could be allocated' (Webb, 1994, p. 58). Consequently, responsibility for these 'left over' subjects could only be given to those who already had curriculum responsibilities or left dormant until a suitable appointment could be made. Though ERA increased the number of art coordinators, the chronology of the introduction of the Statutory Orders did little to raise either their seniority or status.

The place of art coordinators (in common with other coordinators) within the formal authority structures of primary schools varies. Coordination can be (and is) undertaken by any member of staff: headteacher, deputy, experienced or newly qualified teacher. Some coordinators receive above scale allowances for their responsibilities; some do not. Clement (1994) indicates that some 30 per cent of art coordinators in his study — mostly in larger primary schools — held a responsibility allowance for their work.

There is no doubt that some positions in schools offer considerably more favourable opportunities for coordination work than others. It is interesting to compare the access to classrooms (essential if coordinators really are to monitor the curriculum in action) afforded to a headteacher or deputy with few teaching responsibilities with that available to a newly qualified teacher with full class teaching commitments holding similar curriculum responsibilities. This is not to equate 'position' with 'quality' of coordination or to imply, for example that deputy headteachers necessarily possess more developed curriculum leadership qualities than their teaching colleagues (Alexander, 1992).

This differential is particularly significant in the case of art. Alexander identified disturbing links between curriculum leadership, gender and status within the primary schools in his Leeds Survey. He reports that 'mathematics had the highest concentration of senior staff involved in curriculum leadership' (p. 35), then language (though language did not have as many headteachers and deputy headteachers as leaders as mathematics). Art and music, on the other hand, were mainly led by main professional grade teachers. Similar patterns appeared concerning gender in relation to the overall male/female staffing ratios in primary schools. 'Mathematics, computing and environmental studies were disproportionately covered by men, while language, art, music and science were mainly covered by women' (*ibid.*).

As Alexander indicates, this situation provides much food for thought. If institutional power (and attendant decision-making on such matters as resources) is concentrated more in some subject areas than others, what messages does that convey about the value of particular subjects in the eyes of senior managers? (This is particularly important for the arts, given the conclusion of the Gulbenkian Report (Calouste Gulbenkian Foundation, 1982) that they flourish in primary schools where they are clearly appreciated and supported by headteachers and suffer where they are marginalized.) Are particular subject responsibilites more likely to bring promotion? What signals are being given to pupils about which subjects are worthwhile? All are significant questions and not without their own irony, given the place of art in the rhetoric of primary education.

A Position in Search of a Role?

The relationship between coordinators' activities and those of headteachers and deputies has still to be clarified and located satisfactorily within the management structures of schools. The implementation of the National Curriculum and LMS indicated the need to reframe the respective roles of headteachers and deputies in school management, leadership and development (Southworth, 1994; Morrison, 1995). The equally pressing need to rethink the contribution of coordinators to these processes has been neglected, though there is no shortage of advice on what their responsibilities should include.

Organizationally, coordinators — now to be known as 'subject managers'

(OFSTED, 1994c, p. 9) — are to make up the executive arm of the curriculum leadership functions of the headteacher, particularly in monitoring teaching, learning and assessment. They are expected to:

- develop a clear view of the nature of their subject and its contribution to the wider curriculum of the school;
- provide advice and documentation to help teachers to teach the subject and interrelate its constituent elements;
- play a major part in organising the teaching and resources of the subject so that statutory requirements are covered;
- contribute to the overall evaluation of work in their subject against agreed criteria, to evaluate standards of achievement; and to identify trends and patterns in pupils' performance. (*ibid.*)

These OFSTED expectations are embedded in the Handbook for the Inspection of Schools (OFSTED, 1994b) and Guidance on the Inspection of Nursery & Primary Schools (OFSTED, 1995b). Coordinators are required to have an informed view of the quality of teaching and learning in their subject together with a knowledge of pupil achievement. Consequently, they are key players in the inspection process, providing evidence on a range of aspects of school performance such as trends in pupil attainment, management and administration, resources for learning and pupils' behaviour (Howarth and Jelly, 1994). The advantage to schools in beginning to define their own quality assurance expectations of coordinators is not just that senior managers have a means to satisfy these external demands for performance data. More importantly, managers also have the basis for planning development, and, by encouraging and supporting the cycle of reviewing, planning, monitoring, evaluating and reviewing, real opportunities to promote institutional improvement (OFSTED, 1994a). Accountability and professional development are compatible (Cuttance, 1994).

The proposition that coordinators may find their whole-school identity by becoming significant figures in quality assurance begs two questions. First, *what will be required of coordinators to fulfil this role?* There is some evidence to suggest that teachers are likely to need considerable support in developing the necessary skills and understandings; that classroom observation, power relationships (a significant matter for art coordinators) and the adoption of new and unfamiliar language in discussing classroom practice are all likely to be problematic (Humphrey, 1994). Second, *what will schools need to do in order to incorporate quality assurance processes into their managerial ecology?* Not surprisingly, time will be an issue. More time is required, but more time of itself is not the answer. Senior managers will have to consider the distinction made by OFSTED (1994c) between those evaluative activities for which release from other duties is essential — 'monitoring of teaching, learning and assessment practices' (*ibid.*) — and those for which it is not. The comparative failure of school self evaluation so far seems to lie as much in its extensive demands on time as in teachers' lack of the analytical skills necessary to carry it out (Cuttance, 1994).

Predictably, given the general lack of institutional support and resources for these activities in primary schools, there is little evidence that art coordinators have been able to develop their monitoring and evaluating of the art curriculum or contribute in a systematic manner to quality assurance systems. As yet, these aspects of their work have been minimal and remain largely peripheral to the mainstream of primary school management (OFSTED, 1995a).

The Future

The introduction of ERA raised the profile of coordinators and increased their responsibilities without adequately defining their place within the management structure of primary schools. Such integration could be achieved through the establishment of systematic quality assurance processes which allow coordinators to contribute meaningfully to school development. In this way, their subject expertise, classroom practice in art and management planning for improvement may be synthesized.

If art coordinators really are to play a key role in promoting the whole-school development a number of nettles will have to be grasped by teachers, the coordinators themselves, senior managers in schools and central government.

A clear view of what is required to become a coordinator is long overdue. At the moment, no particular attributes appear to be necessary and certainly no consistent, nationally agreed professional competences or attributes are required to be demonstrated before taking on the role. Subject expertise has not been of paramount importance. For example, few art coordinators hold specialist qualifications in art, though the majority appear to have a particular interest in the subject (OFSTED, 1995a). Coordinating responsibilities are too often allocated by a combination of goodwill, persuasion and arm-twisting; understandable given the need to 'cover' all areas of the basic curriculum from within the staffing resources typically available to primary schools (Osborn and Black, 1994).

Change is on the way. At the time of writing, the Secretary of State has defined expectations of newly qualified teachers (NQTs) in terms of course exit performance competences (DFE, 1993b). The Teacher Training Agency (TTA) is developing a career entry profile based on these competences, intended to identify professional strengths and areas for further professional development on entry to the profession. The profile is designed to provide the basis for planned induction support and seems likely to place considerable emphasis on subject knowledge (TTA, 1994).

The TTA, through its Headteacher's Leadership and Management Programme (HEADLAMP), has already identified competences to be developed by newly appointed headteachers (TTA, 1995). It is not difficult to imagine that the next step could be the identification of competences (defined as expectations or attributes) expected of those teachers undertaking curriculum leadership responsibilities. These could include enhancing subject expertise; developing whole-school perspectives on curriculum planning; increasing confidence in encouraging independent pupil learning; dealing with external agencies; communicating with the local community; working effectively with professional colleagues and becoming more proficient in assessing pupil achievement and standards of work across the primary years. Coordination may then begin to attract recognizable career status.

Even if the professional position of coordination within an institution is confirmed in this way, quality assurance in practice is unlikely to be easy. Robust review may well lead to legitimate criticism of management practices — a real difficulty in a primary school. Considerable tensions may be created if, for example, quality in a subject area is being inhibited by the actions of senior management. This is particularly significant when the focus of coordinators' personal appraisal is likely to include subject performance.

Matters of status, power and influence are likely to crystallize in the search for quality in curriculum planning. In order to make the post-Dearing curriculum manageable and meet the statutory requirement that skills, knowledge and understanding in art are systematically developed at Key Stages 1 and 2, schools may be moving to a position where coherence and progression cannot be negotiated by individual teachers. The advice of art coordinators may no longer be regarded as arbitrary (Stannard, 1995). Such a shift will have considerable implications for the culture of primary schools, especially in those where coordinators have been expected to operate solely through persuasion and by invitation.

The future agenda for coordinators will be shaped by the decisions of central government about primary school inspection. Art coordinators' status could be confirmed or diminished by a change in priorities such as an increased emphasis on the inspection of core at the expense of the foundation subject areas. However, it is unlikely that their role in monitoring and evaluating the curriculum will cease to be a major expectation.

The most potent challenge to art coordinators may come from current pressures for semi-specialist and specialist teaching. That challenge is linked to the decisions that schools must make for themselves about their quality assurance processes. For those schools in which quality assurance is synonymous with satisfying external inspection and which see no need to own the process or systematically exploit its potential for whole-school development, responsibilites for standards may be given over, quite legitimately, to named individual coordinators. They carry the can. On the other hand, those schools who do wish to *own* their quality assurance and to distinguish these internal processes from those of external inspection whilst recognizing their reciprocity, may wish to utilize the expertise of their art coordinators in a more collaborative manner. For them, quality assurance is a whole-school, not an individual, matter. The curriculum is a collective responsibility (Campbell, 1985).

Should coordinators be replaced by semi-specialist or specialist teachers there is a real possibility that wider professional learning opportunities will be denied both to coordinators themselves and to their colleagues. If the primary curriculum is delivered entirely through subject teaching there is little necessity for expertise to be shared or the quality of the curriculum as a whole and classroom pedagogy to be a matter of common concern or whole-school debate. Monitoring, evaluation and review need only inform individual subject performance, not collaborative improvement.

If coordinators do not have a distinct contribution to make to colleagues' professional learning, then the prospect of their demise is of no great concern (Edwards, 1993). There is little left in the role that cannot be replaced by specialist teaching. Crucially, a quality assurance system which is clearly linked to whole-school development may be rather more than a means of locating art coordination within primary school management structures — it may be the only means of preserving it.

References

ABBS, P. (1987) *Living Powers*, London, Falmer Press.

ALEXANDER, R. (1992) *Policy and Practice in Primary Education*, London, Routledge.

AUBREY, C. (1994a) 'Overview of advances in understanding of learning and teaching of subject knowledge' in AUBREY, C. (Ed) *The Role of Subject Knowledge in the Early Years of Schooling*, London, Falmer Press.

AUBREY, C. (Ed) (1994b) *The Role of Subject Knowledge in the Early Years of Schooling*, London, Falmer Press.

BUDGE, D. (1995) 'Primaries squeezing the arts into tight corners', *Times Education Supplement*, 6 October.

BUSH, T. (1993) *Exploring Collegiality: Theory and Practice. Unit 2, E326, Module 1, Managing Educational Change*, Milton Keynes, Open University Press.

CALOUSTE GULBENKIAN FOUNDATION (1982) *The Arts in Schools: Principles, Practice and Provision*, London, Calouste Gulbenkian Foundation.

CAMPBELL, R.J. (1985) *Developing the Primary School Curriculum*, London, Holt.

CAMPBELL, R.J. and NEILL, S.R. (1994) *Primary Teachers at Work*, London, Routledge.

CLEMENT, R. (1993) *The Readiness of Primary Schools to Teach the National Curriculum in Art*, Exmouth, The Centre for the Study of the Arts in Primary Education, University of Plymouth.

CLEMENT, R. (1994) 'The readiness of primary schools to teach the National Curriculum in art and design', *Journal of Art and Design Education*, **13**, 1, pp. 9–21.

CUTTANCE, P. (1994) 'The contribution of quality assurance reviews to development in school systems' in HARGREAVES, D. and HOPKINS, D. (Eds) *Development Planning for School Improvement*, London, Cassell.

DES (1978) *Primary Education in England: A Survey by HM Inspectors of Schools*, London, HMSO.

DES (1987) *School Teachers' Pay and Conditions Document*, London, HMSO.

DES (1990) *National Curriculum Art Working Group: Interim Report*, London, HMSO.

DFE (1993a) *Effective Management in Schools*, London, HMSO.

DFE (1993b) *The Initial Training of Primary School Teachers: New Criteria for Courses: (Circular 14/93)* London, DFE.

EDWARDS, A. (1993) 'Curriculum co-ordination: A lost opportunity for primary school development?', *School Organisation*, **13**, 1, pp. 51–9.

HARGREAVES, D. and HOPKINS, D. (1994) *Development Planning for School Improvement*, London, Cassell.

HARRISON, M. (Ed) (1995) *Developing a Leadership Role in Key Stage 2 Curriculum*, London, Falmer Press.

HOWARTH, S. and JELLY, S. (1994) 'Asking the impossible? OFSTED expectations of subject managers in primary schools', *Management in Education*, **8**, 4, p. 9.

HUMPHREY, K. (1994) 'My ball, your game: Dilemmas in self-regulation according to the OFSTED criteria', *British Journal of In — service Education*, **20**, 2, pp. 181–93.

KELLY, V. (1995) *Education and Democracy*, London, Paul Chapman Publishing.

MORRISON, K. (1995) 'The deputy headteacher as the leader of the curriculum in primary schools', *School Organisation*, **15**, 1, pp. 65–76.

NCC (1993) *Planning the National Curriculum at Key Stage 2*, York, NCC.

OFSTED (1994a) *Improving Schools*, London, HMSO.

OFSTED (1994b) *The Handbook for the Inspection of Schools*, London, HMSO.

OFSTED (1994c) *Primary Matters*, London, OFSTED.

OFSTED (1995a) *Art: A Review of Inspection Findings 1993/94*, London, HMSO.

OFSTED (1995b) *The OFSTED Handbook: Guidance on the Inspection of Nursery & Primary Schools*, London, HMSO.

OSBORN, M. and BLACK, E. (1994) *Developing the National Curriculum at Key Stage 2: The Changing Nature of Teachers' Work*, Bristol, Centre for Curriculum and Assessment Studies School of Education, University of Bristol.

PIOTROWSKI, J. (1995) 'Coordinating the art curriculum at Key Stage 2' in HARRISON, M. (Ed) *Developing a Leadership Role in Key Stage 2 Curriculum*, London, Falmer Press.

SCAA (1995) *Planning the National Curriculum at Key Stages 1 and 2*, London, SCAA.

SOUTHWORTH, G. (1994) 'Two heads are better than one', *Managing Schools Today*, **4**, 3, pp. 3–6.

STANNARD, J. (1995) 'Managing the primary curriculum after Dearing: A rationale', *Education 3–13*, **23**, 1, pp. 3–7.

TAYLOR, R. and ANDREWS, G. (1993) *The Arts in the Primary School*, London, Falmer Press.

TTA (1994) *Profiles of Teacher Competence — Consultation on Draft Guidance*, London, TTA.

TTA (1995) *HEADLAMP: Headteacher Leadership and Management Programme Procedures*, London, TTA.

WEBB, R. (1994) *After the Deluge: Changing Roles and Responsibilities in the Primary School*, London, Association of Teachers and Lecturers.

6   Hidden Strengths: The Case for the Generalist Teacher of Art

David Holt

Introduction

During the process of intense and rapid change which has characterized the education system in recent times, much attention has — quite properly — been paid to examining the overall effectiveness of primary education. An important aspect of this process has been the emergence of rather more critical attitudes towards methods of curriculum organization and delivery which have previously been regarded as being central to the very idea of good primary education.

One such practice is strongly challenged by Alexander, Rose and Woodhead (1992), who present a strong critique of previously unquestioned methods of curriculum organization and delivery within the primary school. In particular, the widespread use of generalist teachers to deliver the whole of the primary curriculum is identified as highly problematical. In many cases, it is suggested, such an approach is likely to work against the achievement of high standards in the subjects, particularly given the heavy demands of the National Curriculum at Key Stage 1 and Key Stage 2. Whilst sensibly acknowledging the need for primary teachers to develop a wider 'curricular expertise' — a notion which is taken to include 'understanding how children learn, and the skills needed to teach subjects sucessfully' — the centrality of subject knowledge within this idea is uncompromisingly asserted:

> Opinion is divided about the relative importance of the teacher's sub-ject knowledge . . . Our own view is that subject knowledge is a criti-cal factor at every point in the teaching process: in planning, assessing and diagnosing, task setting, questioning, explaining and giving feed-back. The key question to be answered is whether the class teacher system makes impossible demands on the subject knowledge of the generalist primary teacher. We believe that it does . . . (para. 77)

As a result of this alleged weakness in generalist teaching, it is suggested that much greater consideration should be given to the use of subject specialists, particularly at the upper end of the primary age phase. Superficially, no doubt, such an idea would appear to have a great deal to commend it, particularly given the subject-based nature of the National Curriculum, and the extent to which this represents a significant shift from the rather looser, topic and person centred approach that previously characterized much of primary education. Similarly, it is clear that many schools and teachers have experienced significant problems with the implementation of the new curriculum (Campbell and Neill, 1994), and the move to specialist teaching might therefore appear to offer a quick and easy way out of such difficulties. Clearly, given contemporary political anxieties over the raising of standards and the delivery of what is effectively a secondary-style curriculum at primary level, such views are likely to exert a significant effect upon future developments within the overall field of primary education. Indeed, there are already some indications that this could indeed be the case. Without doubt, much of the report's value structure appears to be reflected in emerging developments concerned with teacher training, where an increasing emphasis is being placed upon the development of students' abilities to function in a specialist capacity (DES, 1993). Similarly, it may also be apparent in comments made during a recent lecture by Her Majesty's Chief Inspector of Schools, criticizing what is described as the 'unhelpful influence' of 'progressive' methods (Hackett, 1995).

Whilst Alexander, Rose and Woodhead (1992) are obviously concerned with the whole of the primary curriculum, this chapter will be rather more focused in its concerns. In accordance with my own professional concerns and the orientation of this book, it will examine the significance of what the report has to say with particular regard to the practice of generalist art teaching in primary schools.

The sort of criticism of traditional primary approaches to curriculum delivery that is identified above is an inevitable consequence of the imposition of a subject-based National Curriculum. Without doubt, the basic structure and approach of this initiative clearly makes very little concession to the range of pressing educational, developmental and logistical considerations which necessarily influence the ways in which primary schools typically choose to go about their work. However, whilst the idea of a radical shift to widespread specialist teaching at primary level may or may not be a sensible objective for teachers and administrators to consider, it is at least arguable as to whether it represents one that stands any realistic chance of actually being achieved. Certainly, it seems entirely unlikely that any government — of whatever persuasion — would welcome the very substantial risks that would seem to be associated with the adoption of such a policy.

Some of these would be political, in that a global change of this nature would necessarily dictate the closing down or amalgamation of large numbers of smaller schools, many of which would undoubtedly be situated in rural areas of great electoral sensitivity. Others would be economic, in the sense that the process would inevitably be extremely expensive, and likely to remain so over a prolonged period. Finally, there would undoubtedly be the potential for substantial problems with the teaching profession. Firstly, there must be some considerable doubt as to whether there would actually be enough specialist understanding available — and in the right places — within the primary schools in order to resource such a change of approach. More significantly, however, it is clear that support for both generalist and integrated approaches remains extremely high amongst primary practitioners (Galton, 1995). Accordingly, any attempt to impose what would undoubtedly be seen by such teachers as a largely alien and inappropriate system would certainly run the risk of provoking a substantial reaction of the kind last seen with regard to testing in schools.

However, if a general move to specialist teaching within the primary school seems unlikely, then a rather more gradual approach would also appear to be fraught with difficulty. Even if this were to be attempted — perhaps by making use of peripatetic teachers — it would seem highly unlikely that such an expensive solution would be applied to a subject like art. This has already been marginalized, not only by traditional public perceptions of the subject, but also by its current location outside the core of the National Curriculum, and by its removal from the mandatory post-14 curriculum. Additionally, if such a peripatetic system were to be set up, the troubled history of similar approaches to the teaching of music in primary schools indicates just what a vulnerable solution this would represent in troubled economic times.

Given that there appears to be good reason to suppose that generalist teaching will continue to be a common feature of primary education for the foreseeable future, this chapter will suggest that rather more consideration needs to be given to the approach as it impacts upon the teaching of art. In general, it will represent a defence of the generalist system, although it will by no means ignore the problems which are sometimes associated with its use. Nevertheless, the overall approach will be essentially positive. Firstly, it will suggest that at primary level, although the importance of subject knowledge cannot be denied, its significance is currently being somewhat overstated. Next, it will argue that the generalist approach offers a number of clear advantages to the teaching of art, which educators in this area of the curriculum would be ill advised, either to ignore, or to minimize. Finally, it will attempt to look at the weaknesses of generalist art teaching as they have been identified over the years, and give some consideration to ways in which these might be minimized and the potential advantages of the approach be more widely realized in practice.

The Significance of Subject Knowledge

Quite properly, Alexander, Rose and Woodhead (1992) identify the central importance of subject knowledge within all effective teaching. However, the undoubted significance of such knowledge should not be exaggerated. Clearly, it is quite quite impossible for anyone to teach anything unless they have sufficient knowledge about the subject in question. However, it is equally apparent that, beyond a certain necessary minimum — which must be a function of the level at which the teaching is undertaken — the possession of subject knowledge of itself offers absolutely no guarantee of quality. Indeed, at all levels of education, it is quite possible to identify teachers who, although extremely knowledgeable in their subjects, are nevertheless quite unable, either to teach these coherently, or to motivate their pupils to learn in the area concerned. This is by no means an unusual phenomenon, and most educated people will have their own painful memories of such unfortunate encounters within their own educational experience.

Consequently, it would appear far too simple to suggest that a change to specialist teaching in the primary school would inevitably lead to a wholesale raising of standards. In some cases, no doubt, that might indeed be the result; but in others, there would almost certainly be no such effect. Where things did improve, it seems unlikely that the quantity of subject knowledge involved would be the significant issue. This would, presumably, be more or less the same for all specialists, and so some other factor, perhaps to be found in that wider notion of 'curriculum expertise' raised by Alexander, Rose and Woodhead (1992), would be at work. Thus, to argue that there is necessarily a direct and proportionate relationship between the level of a teacher's subject knowledge, and the quality of their teaching, would seem to be a highly misleading assumption.

Of course, this is not to imply that, where primary teachers are concerned, there is not a need for them to develop deeper levels of knowledge and understanding about art, and the possibility of achieving this will be returned to later in this discussion. However, it is to suggest that, providing that they can be helped to acquire the necessary irriducible minimum level of subject knowledge identified above, then it is possible to argue that generalist teaching can offer significant advantages to the teaching of art in the primary school, and these will now be examined.

Possible Advantages of Generalist Art Teaching

Managing Developmental Transition

Any successful system of primary art education must be capable of ensuring that children gain adequate levels of confidence and competence within this area of the curriculum. However, it is also clear that, in emotional terms, the experience of making art within school is, at particular times, likely to be deeply difficult for many — perhaps most — children. This is because, when properly undertaken, the activity inevitably involves the making of images of a deeply personal and expressive nature within the highly public social context that is the classroom. As a result, it is entirely unsurprising that the experience frequently carries with it the possibility of individuals feeling of isolated, vulnerable and inadequate as a result of their involvement with such activity.

In the early stages of education, there is not likely to be much of a problem in this regard. It is entirely characteristic of young children, who are likely still to be in the initial stages of their social and intellectual development, to adopt a consistently egocentric attitude towards their art work, and they are consequently likely to be relatively indifferent to the kinds of pressures described above. However, it is clear that this innocence does not last for very long. As children pass into later childhood, they experience what one writer (Gentle, 1985) has graphically described as 'a second shock to the development of mind', which finally removes them from the self-centredness which has previously protected them from the more threatening aspects of the practice of art. As a consequence of this, and of the increasing socialization which comes with it, the child becomes uncomfortably aware of the existence of viewpoints, standards and opinions that exist outside itself. Additionally, it also begins to comprehend the difference between these phenomena and its own work. As a result, the child's response to image making is thrown into crisis:

> Seven is often referred to as the age of self awareness. It is the age where there is a curiosity about experience, about things, people, events and places. This leads the child to realise that the way he sees the world and how it actually is are two different things. He also becomes aware that he sees, feels and knows differently from others. (p. 21)

Obviously, such a crisis marks a critical point in the child's development. However, it also just as clearly represents a challenge to the teaching of art within the primary school. If wrongly handled, the problem can all too easily lead on to the phenomenon characterized as the 'shrinking artist' (Barnes, 1989), in which the child's growing frustration with, and loss of, interest in art eventually culminates in near complete withdrawal from the activity. This decline is often exacerbated by parents, who, aware of their children's problem with art, actively encourage it in order to concentrate their work upon what are seen as more 'important' educational activities. This phenomenon has also been registered by others in this field. For example, Clement (1990) notes the likelihood of children suffering a terminal loss of confidence at this stage unless they are provided with appropriate levels and forms of support by their teachers:

> It is all too easy at this stage for children to lose their confidence in their ability and to decide that 'I'm no good at art' or 'I can't draw'. (p. 14)

In much the same way, Morgan (1988) points to the danger of children becoming 'disillusioned' with earlier art work, and indicates the need for sensitive and informed teaching in order to support them during this difficult period. Similarly, Rubens and Newland (1989) identify the need for pupils who are caught within this problematical situation to receive active assistance from teachers:

> The learner needs at this stage, to be helped towards an awareness
> that there are always a number of 'right' solutions to each problem . . .
> The teacher's task is, as always, to assist the learner's autonomous
> development. (p. 11)

The significance of all this to the practice of generalist teaching is not hard to
discern. Given that all children within the primary school are likely to pass
through this developmental crisis at some point, there is plainly a need for
them to be helped through the experience. At one level, this need is clearly
practical, in the sense that, if good quality support in the use of materials and
processes is not made available, then the child's art education is unlikely to
progress very much further. However, there is another aspect to the problem,
which is emotional rather than practical. Clearly, the kind of crisis that is being
considered here is necessarily involved with substantial issues of confidence
and self esteem. As a result, in addition to formal 'teaching', children encountering such problems with their work in art also need to receive a degree of
emotional support if they are to cope with a situation that is perceived as
inherently threatening. Clearly, such support is likely to be most effective
when it it is provided by somebody the children concerned both know and
trust, and who also knows them very well. Given that generalist teachers are
likely to have the closest of relationships with the children whom they teach,
it seems entirely reasonable to conclude that they are are likely to be better
placed than a visiting specialist teacher to provide the quality of support that
will help pupils through this difficult time.

Developing Pupil Understanding of the Nature and Purposes of Art

However, art education at primary level must also be concerned with developing pupils' understanding of art in a way that is appropriate to their age and
stage of development. The development of such understanding is clearly important, not only in a general educational sense, but also in terms of the
precise demands of the National Curriculum. For example, the requirement
within the Programmes of Study that children at Key Stages 1 and 2 'should be
given opportunities to develop understanding of the work of artists, craftspeople
and designers' must necessarily involve them in coming to know something
about the reasons why artists do what they do.

Before the advent of the National Curriculum, primary children's understanding of the nature and purposes of art as a cultural phenomenon was not
really an issue. In those days, the focus of most art education for young
children was apparently rather more concerned with the provision of a wide
variety of experiences with different materials. However, this approach was
apparently not without problems for teachers. The Plowden Report (CACE,
1967), which was apparently largely satisfied with the standard of primary
school art 'at its best', also took care to note that there was 'no cause for

complacency' (p. 248), and as time went on, the situation clearly deteriorated. Dixon (1976) identifies the difficulty and superficiality of much generalist art teaching of the time:

> the teachers tended to find great difficulty in presenting new things for their children to do. There was a man called Henry Pluckrose who seemed to think up lots of things for them to try and a monthly art and craft magazine which supposedly contained lots of good ideas. (p. 75)

This novelty-based approach to art teaching was clearly not restricted to the United Kingdom. Eisner (1972) identifies a similar methodology prevailing in American elementary education at this time, which he associates with a heavy emphasis on the provision of an impossibly wide variety of materials and processes, justified on the grounds that diversity of this kind is necessarily stimulating. Barkan (1962) makes the nature of this conceptual confusion (Holt, 1989) very clear indeed. In particular, he notes the tendency for such teachers to judge the quality of their art teaching on the basis of quantity, rather than quality:

> The more media they provide, the better they think they are teaching; the more varieties of media their children experience, the better they assume the learning to be . . . Most of them are on a perpetual hunt for not only for more media but also for new ones. (p. 16)

The development of children's conceptual understanding of art — as opposed to the provision of a wide but essentially unfocused and decontextualized experience of art materials and processes — was apparently unimportant for popular approaches to primary art education during this period. However, the same is plainly not true today. As has already been noted, the current requirements of the National Curriculum expect that children will begin to develop not only some understanding of the use of materials and processes, but also an ability to make use of these in order to respond to and make sense of significant personal experience. Thus, the Programmes of Study for Attainment Target 1 at Key Stage 1, require that pupils should 'record what has been experienced, observed and imagined'. At Key Stage 2 there is a related expectation that they use such material more selectively for individual purposes. Similarly, the Programmes of Study at Key Stages 1 and 2 both require that pupils should respond to 'the ideas, methods or approaches used in different styles and traditions' of art, but at an increasingly sophisticated level in Key Stage 2. Thus, the overall aim of art education in the primary school may be seen as having shifted from the unstructured experiencing of materials that was earlier described. Instead, it is now concerned with the development of a rather deeper practical and conceptual understanding of this area of the curriculum. This includes not only the achievement of competence in a limited number of defined practical activities such as drawing, painting, printmaking, collage and sculpture, but also the development of some degree of under-standing of the purposes of art within the context of human experience.

If primary children are to come to understand that art is necessarily con-cerned with responding to significant personal experience, then there are clearly some implications for the manner in which such work is initiated within the classroom. For example, wherever possible, it would seem important that art activities should be based upon experiences that have in some way 'moved' the children. This term is used here to signify any meaningful emotional re-sponse that is generated in children by their experiences, and may therefore be understood to include considerations such as excitement, interest, curiosity, wonder, and so on. In other words, experience that 'moves' children is any-thing that makes a significant emotional impression upon them, and which therefore provides a chance for them to respond expressively through the use of expressive materials (Witkin, 1974). In this way, it becomes possible for children to begin to have some experience of working like artists, and thus begin to develop a much deeper understanding of the nature of the activity.

If this is so, it clearly becomes necessary for the primary teacher of art to have a clear view of exactly where pupils' interests and excitements lie at any given moment, for it is these areas that are likely to provide the best oppor-tunities for the generation of significant art work. Clearly, generalists are in a position of considerable advantage in this respect. At any given time, they are highly likely to have a good idea of both the state and the nature of their children's enthusiasms. This is not only because of their close and continuing relationship with the children that they teach. It is also because they will almost certainly have generated many of these interests themselves as a result of their own teaching elsewhere in the curriculum. Additionally, the close personal knowledge which generalists inevitably develop about individual children will also mean that they are often able to identify 'private' interests which might similarly form the basis for meaningful art activity.

Managing Curriculum Time Effectively

In common with other subject areas, there is necessarily a relationship be-tween the practice of art and the achievement of quality. Because the practice of art necessarily involves the shaping of expressive materials in order to make sense of ideas and feelings (*ibid.*; Ross, 1978), it must also involve a thinking, as well as a practical, process. One of the objectives of art education in the primary school must therefore be to help children understand this important aspect of the activity.

The nature of art as an essentially reflexive process is certainly implicit within the National Curriculum, where it is clearly expected that children will begin to develop some understanding of the process of dialogue that neces-sarily exists, both within and between individual pieces of art work. For ex-ample, the Programme of Study for Attainment Target 1 at Key Stage 1 makes this clear, in that pupils are expected to be able to 'review what they have done and describe what they might change in future work'. At Key Stage 2, this understanding is built and developed somewhat further, when pupils are required to keep a sketchbook, and also be able to 'reflect on and adapt their work in the light of what they intended and consider what they might develop in future work'. The requirement for such progression clearly signals a concern with the achievement of quality, not only as regards the use of materials, but also where the thinking processes art is concerned. However, the achievement of such learning is necessarily predicated upon the availability of sufficient time for this complex process to take place. By definition, art work — being concerned with the achievement of quality — cannot be hurried if it is to achieve its educational purposes, and there must clearly be time for thought and contingent action to take place.

Here, the primary generalist is, once again, quite clearly in an extremely strong position. Unless constrained by what would be, even by today's anxious standards, uncharacteristically rigid timetabling, it is clearly possible for such teachers to manage the total amount of time available within the curriculum in such a way as to provide enough for children to be able to develop the kind of quality response discussed above. Of course, this does not imply any attempt to gain more time for art at the expense of other subjects. Despite the recent Dearing Review, the curriculum still appears to be somewhat overloaded, and to take such a line would clearly be wholly unrealistic. However, what can be done so well by the generalist is the manipulation of what curriculum time is available in such a way that it is offered to children in a more concentrated and more appropriate forms. This, of course, may well mean losing the longstanding primary view of art as a weekly entitlement. However, the educational benefits of fewer, but necessarily more intense and productive art sessions might well prove to be worthy of such a sacrifice.

Problematical Aspects of Generalist Art Teaching

Despite what appear to be genuine potential strengths in the teaching of art by generalists within the primary school, it is important to be realistic. In the past, it is clear that there have been widespread and significant problems associated with this approach to art teaching as it has actually operated within the schools. Indeed, during the period between the publication of the generally optimistic Plowden Report and the rather more cautionary account of arts education provided by Gulbenkian Foundation (1982), a pattern of growing concern about the quality of such work gradually becomes apparent. This concern is to be seen in the increasingly negative judgments made by a series of national investigations (DES, 1971, 1978a and 1982a) all of which are concerned with the quality of art education in primary schools. These official documents consistently identify a number of substantial difficulties associated with the teaching of art by generalist teachers.

Most importantly, these are concerned with an apparent lack of achievement by pupils at the upper end of the primary age range, poor quality of teaching and a profound and widespread lack of confidence amongst generalist teachers. With regard to the latter point, a range of other sources identify the confusion that is apparent amongst many generalists operating within this subject area. The nature of this growing perception of a crisis in primary art teaching is perhaps enunciated most clearly in the 1978 Schools Council Bulletin:

> There is a genuine belief amongst art educators that the last decade has seen something of a decline in the quality and purpose of work in art in the 7–11 age range.

However, whilst there undoubtedly much within the literature of this area to reinforce this predominantly negative impression, it is also necessary to register that there is also an alternative, and more optimistic view. This is to be found in an admittedly smaller, but nonetheless extremely persuasive body of material which clearly presents a very different view. For example, work by Marshall (1963) and Armstrong (1980) provide specific accounts of generalist practice, all of which indicate the high quality of art work that is possible within such situations. On a somewhat wider level, at least one official publication (DES, 1978b) celebrates the quality of art work being undertaken at the time by a number of junior schools and departments. Much more recently, a detailed account of quality generalist art teaching has been provided by Clement and Tarr (1992), who follow the work undertaken by a single primary school during a school year. Additionally, in the period around the introduction of the National Curriculum, a number of accounts of good practice in primary art education have been published (Barnes, 1989; Morgan, 1988; Clement and Page, 1992a, b and c). All of these provide clear documentary evidence to support the contention that good generalist art teaching is not only possible, but is actually occurring in some primary schools.

Conclusion

It has been argued that generalist teaching can offer a number of significant advantages to the teaching of art within the primary school, and that these are capable of leading to higher standards of learning and achievement within the subject. These advantages are to be found in the suitability of such teachers to offer appropriate emotional support to children passing through difficult and painful developmental transitions; in the way in which their necessarily deeper knowledge of the children they teach renders it easier for them to make classroom work more reflective of the nature of art by relating it to the current interests of the pupils involved, and the relative ease with which they can deploy curriculum time more effectively to maximize the chances of pupils achieving the quality of response which good art education necessarily demands.

That such quality of teaching is achievable within the primary sector is entirely clear. Even from the small amount of evidence that has been considered, it is quite clear that there are reasonable grounds for supposing that recent practice in schools is much improved. This view is clearly supported by a recent official pronouncement concerned with standards in the teaching of art (OFSTED, 1993), which describes 68 per cent of art lessons at Key Stage 1 as being at a level judged to be 'satisfactory or better'. At Key Stage 2, the figure is admittedly rather lower at 58 per cent. The majority of teachers concerned are characterized as 'working hard', but their limited experience with materials and lack of knowledge of the subject are identified as being problematical. Clearly, whilst matters may be improving, there is still some way to go.

The reason for the continuation of such problems is probably not too hard to find. There can be little doubt that the origins of shortcomings in this area are largely located in the manner in which teachers destined for primary schools are prepared for their role as generalists. Until recently, teacher education has either chosen — or been obliged — to organize courses in which students have spent the major part of their time in the study of a single subject. Even before the major curriculum reforms introduced by the 1988 Act, and the increased emphasis which these placed upon teachers' subject knowledge, this had appeared to be a somewhat idiosyncratic way of preparing generalists. However, since the Education Reform Act, the approach has come to seem increasingly irrelevant. This, of course, is not to imply that there is not a need for primary practitioners to develop a particular strength and interest in a specific area of the curriculum. This is obviously significant, both in terms of personal development and professional usefulness. However, it is to suggest that the squandering of so much time in the study of a single subject has, for many years, inevitably undermined the proper preparation of generalists. As a result, such students have typically received only a minimal preparation for the teaching of their non-specialist subjects like art (DES, 1982b; Sharp, 1990). Accordingly, it is not surprising that there have been so many difficulties associated with primary teachers' lack of knowledge and understanding in this area of the curriculum. Fortunately, with the recent emergence of new criteria for teacher education in DFE *Circular 14/93*, the requirement to devote half of a student's total training to a single area has now been removed. As a result, it may at last be possible to develop courses which prepare primary teachers in a more rational and even handed manner, and thus maximize the opportunities of liberating the undoubted potential of the generalist system. Where the quality of art education in the primary school is concerned, there may be much to be gained.

References

ALEXANDER, R., ROSE, J. and WOODHEAD, C. (1992) *Curriculum Organisation and Classroom Practice*, London, HMSO.

ARMSTRONG, M. (1980) *Closely Observed Children*, Oxford, Writers and Readers.

BARKAN, M. (1962) 'Transition in art education', *Art Education*, **15**, 7, pp. 12–18.

BARNES, R. (1989) *Teaching Art to Young Children 4–9*, London, Allen nd Unwin.

CALOUSTE GULBENKIAN FOUNDATION (1982) *The Arts in Schools*, London, Gulbenkian Foundation.

CAMPBELL, J. and NEILL, S. (1994) *Curriculum Reform at Key Stage 1: Teacher Commitment and Policy Failure*, Harlow, Longman.

CACE (1967) *Children and Their Primary Schools*, London, HMSO.

CLEMENT, R. (1990) *A Framework for Art, Craft and Design in the Primary Schools*, Exeter, Devon Education Authority.

CLEMENT, R. and PAGE, S. (1992a) *Principles and Practice in Art*, Harlow, Oliver & Boyd.

CLEMENT, R. and PAGE, S. (1992b) *Investigating and Making in Art*, Harlow, Oliver & Boyd.

CLEMENT, R. and PAGE, S. (1992c) *Knowledge and Understanding in Art*, Harlow, Oliver & Boyd.

CLEMENT, R. and TARR, E. (1992) *A Year in the Art of a Primary School*, Corsham, NSEAD.

DES (1971) *Education Survey Number 11: Art in Schools*, London, HMSO.

DES (1978a) *Primary Education in England*, London, HMSO.

DES (1978b) *Art in Junior Education*, London, HMSO.

DES (1982a) *Education 5–9*, London, HMSO.

DES (1982b) *The New Teacher in School*, London, HMSO.

DES (1993) *The Initial Training of Primary School Teachers* (Circular 14/93) London, HMSO.

DIXON, P. (1976) 'Art and craft — Point and purpose', *Education 3–13*. October, pp. 75–80.

EISNER, E. (1972) *Educating Artistic Vision*, New York, Macmillan.

GALTON, M. (1995) *Crisis in the Primary Classroom*, London, Fulton.

GENTLE, K. (1985) *Children and Art Teaching*, Beckenham, Croom Helm.

HACKETT, G. (1995) 'Woodhead castigates progressives', *Times Educational Supplement*, 27 January.

HOLT, D. (1989) 'Grasping the nettle: The arts in primary education' in Ross, M. (Ed) *The Claims of Feeling*, London, Falmer Press.

MARSHALL, S. (1963) *An Experiment in Education*, Cambridge, Cambridge University Press.

MORGAN, M. (1988) *Art 4–11*, Oxford, Basil Blackwell.

OFSTED (1993) *Art Key Stages 1, 2 and 3, First Year 1992–93: The implementation of the curricular requirements of the Education Reform Act*, London, HMSO.

ROSS, M. (1978) *The Creative Arts*, London, Heinemann Educational Books.

ROSS, M. (Ed) (1989) *The Claims of Feeling*, London, Falmer Press.

RUBENS, M. and NEWLAND, M. (1989) *A Tool for Learning*, Ipswich, Direct Experience.

SCHOOLS COUNCIL (1978) *Art Committee Occasional Bulletin. Art 7–11*, London, Schools Council.

SHARP, C. (1990) *Developing the Arts in Primary Schools: Good Practice in Teacher Education*, Slough, NFER.

WITKIN, R. (1974) *The Intelligence of Feeling*, London, Heinemann.

7 Educating the Human Spirit: an Approach to the Spiritual Dimension of Primary Arts Education

J. Mark Halstead

This all-important spark of inner life today is at present only a spark. Our minds, which are even now only just awakening after years of materialism, are infected with the despair of unbelief, of lack of purpose and ideal. (Kandinsky, 1970, pp. 1–2)

Introduction

The last five or six years have seen a remarkable upsurge of interest in the spiritual dimension of education in Britain. This interest is typically explained (cf. Minney, 1991) by the inclusion in the 1988 Education Act of the requirement that schools should provide 'a broad and balanced curriculum which promotes the spiritual . . . development of pupils at school and of society'. Of course, the term has a much longer history, since the 1944 Education Act speaks of the 'spiritual . . . development of the community'. The theme is developed further in the Newsom Report (Ministry of Education, 1963), which devotes a whole chapter to spiritual and moral development, and in the HMI series *Curriculum Matters* (DES, 1985) which describes the spiritual as one of eight key areas of learning and experience. However, the rapid growth of interest since the early 1990s is probably the result of the coincidence of three factors:

(i)   a growing recognition that many of the current trends in education in Britain (including the emphasis on market values, management styles drawn from business, the preparation of pupils for the workplace, the emphasis on assessable knowledge and skills and an increasingly instrumental conception of the task of teaching) have been at the expense of personal development or the development of character;

(ii) a raising of the profile of traditional and non-traditional forms of spirituality in a variety of contexts throughout — and beyond — the Western world (cf. Halstead, 1994b; Michaud, 1994; Taylor, 1994);

(iii)   a determination by the British Government to highlight the spiritual dimension of education by the requirement of the 1992 Education (Schools) Act that Her Majesty's Chief Inspector of Schools should keep the Secretary of State informed, among other things, about the spiritual development of pupils and by the corresponding requirement that registered inspectors should comment on spiritual development whenever they report on a school inspection.

These three factors have in turn led to increasing attention being paid to the spiritual dimension of education on the part both of Government agencies and of academics and educational researchers in Britain. In 1993, the National Curriculum Council (NCC) circulated a discussion paper on spiritual and moral development (reissued by SCAA, 1995), and the following year OFSTED produced its own discussion paper on spiritual, moral, social and cultural development (OFSTED, 1994). Conferences on the theme have been organized by Westhill College, the University of Plymouth, Homerton College, Roehampton Institute and, in 1996, by SCAA; *SPES*, a magazine devoted mainly to the spiritual dimension of education, has been launched by the University of Plymouth; local education authorities have produced guidance for schools (see, for example, Bradford Inspection and Cultural Services, 1990; Hertfordshire Education Services, 1993); materials and resources are currently being produced by the Christian Education Movement and other organizations for use in schools; and a growing number of academic articles have been written on the topic, several of which are included in the bibliography at the end of this chapter.

Clearly many people believe that all this flurry of activity has something to do with the arts. In their discussion of the spiritual dimension of education, the authors of an HMI series suggest that 'dance, drama, music, art and literature witness to the element of mystery in human experience across the centuries and in every culture' (DES, 1985). In an article in *The Tablet* written when he was Secretary of State for Education and Science, John Patten (1992, p. 1257) refers to the 'spiritual questions' raised by 'inspiring' passages of music or 'uplifting' works of art or literature. Carr (1995) writes that 'one area of the curriculum which does seem to have a strong claim to be a vehicle of spiritual education is that of the arts . . . (since they) have a key part to play in communicating or explicating the sense of a connection between the temporal and the eternal, the finite and the infinite, the material world and the world of the soul, in human affairs' (p. 95).

However, although this kind of token acknowledgment is often made of the connection between the arts and the spiritual dimension of education, there is evidence to suggest that it has little impact on practice. A recent study of forty church schools highlighted the gulf between the perceived importance of the expressive arts in promoting spiritual development and the actual practice in schools. Thirty-one of the schools claimed that the expressive arts 'made a large contribution to spiritual development', while only three made reference to the arts when asked about specific methods used for spiritual development (Hallis, 1995). There may be several reasons for this gap between rhetoric and reality. Few recent books on the arts in education even mention the spiritual dimension, let alone attempt a systematic exploration of it, and teachers of the arts are under such pressures already that without considerable guidance they are unable to launch out onto a new initiative. In any case, the spiritual dimension of education is still in a dreadful mess conceptually, with the result that many people are still to be convinced of its importance.

The present chapter, therefore, seeks to take stock of this under-researched topic and to provide a few pointers along the way. The next section will explore the meaning of the concept 'spiritual' and why it is important in an educational context. The third section will examine the relationship between spirituality and the arts. The final section will be concerned with the ways that a concern for the spiritual development of children may affect the way we understand and approach primary arts education.

Spirituality and Education

The term 'spiritual' is extraordinarily complex and problematic. One set of problems is that it means such different, even contradictory, things to different people. For some, a sexual relationship may be a spiritual experience, but for others it may be the opposite. For some, there may be a deeply spiritual element in a mathematical solution, but for others this may be the antithesis of the spiritual. The spiritual is defined by some as the opposite of the material, the rational, the secular or the physical, whereas others may see it as a dimension of any or all of these. For Mitch Kapor, cofounder of Lotus software, computer technology offers a new path to personal liberation because it represents 'a new spiritual dimension — release from the prison of your own mind' (Taylor, 1994, p. 62). Another set of problems is that the term has sometimes been hijacked by fringe movements; a section in a bookshop labelled 'The Spiritual' is likely to contain books on the paranormal, UFOs, mystical experiences, New Age world views, tarot cards, Satanism and the martial arts. A third set of problems is that the meaning of the term 'spiritual' has changed over time. For many centuries it was used almost exclusively in the context either of religion generally or of the more sacred and devotional aspects of religion, which are sometimes called 'the lived experience of religion' (cf Starkings, 1993, p. 10). However, a recent survey suggests that uses of the term 'spirituality' with a religious meaning are now in the minority; more commonly it is used to describe an aspect of personality, a characteristic ethos or a way of perceiving nature and life (Hull, 1993).

It seems to me that the terms 'spiritual' and 'spirituality' have a chameleon-like quality, changing their hue in accordance with the noun or adjective which accompanies them (such as 'Sioux spirituality', 'spiritual healing', 'spiritual enlightenment' and so on). Thus 'women's spirituality celebrates the 'inward-focused intuitive, imaginal, and relation-oriented powers of women' (Taylor, 1994, p. 66), in contrast to the more rational, controlling and unfeeling male psyche. Combined with 'education', the term 'spiritual' takes on the hue of education, with all that implies in terms of the development of personal auto-nomy, critical openness, the pursuit of truth, respect for others and tolerance of diversity. Versions of spirituality which do not also involve these educational characteristics would be inappropriate goals for the common school. Thus when Jesus says, 'Lay not up for yourselves treasures on earth . . .', he may indeed be pointing to a deep truth about the spiritual life; but the development of the spiritual life in this religious sense cannot be the goal of the common school. The term 'spiritual education' implies different ends.

We have now reached the stage where it is possible to spell out at least some of the conditions which any adequate conceptualization of the term 'spiritual education' must satisfy if it is to have value in the context of the common school:

(i)   It must be in harmony with the values of the broader society, for any education which does not take appropriate account of these values will not prove acceptable to those with a legitimate interest in education.
(ii) It must not be isolated from other aspects of children's development, for the wellbeing of the child can only be approached holistically.
(iii) It must avoid divisiveness, which would go against the spirit of the common school.
(iv) It must be grounded in openness and thus avoid indoctrination or the promotion of specific religious beliefs.

Bearing these criteria in mind, I believe it is most helpful to interpret 'spiritual education' as the *education of the human spirit*, that is, education which is directed towards the development of fundamental human characteristics and capacities such as love, peace, wonder, joy, imagination, hope, forgiveness, integrity, sensitivity, creativity, aspiration, idealism, the search for meaning, values and commitment and the capacity to respond to the challenges of change, hardship, danger, suffering and despair. Elsewhere (Halstead, 1992) I have suggested that this process involves two dimensions:

1   Looking inwards: personal identity and individual development. This includes developing a sense of self and of identity within a group; personality and behaviour; educating the emotions; developing qualities of character; developing the conscience and the will.
2   Looking outwards: some spiritual responses to life. These include creativity; contemplation; personal commitments; the quest for meaning and for something beyond ourselves; living for others (cf. Hull, 1996, p. 43).

Each of the elements within the two dimensions represents a significant aspect of what it is to be human, and pupils should be encouraged to explore the resonances, if any, with their own lives. For some, those resonances will have a distinctively religious or transcendent quality and for others, not. But in the broader sense referring to the development of fundamental human character-istics, the term 'spiritual education' is equally relevant to all. It is an essential part of education, though it has not always been called 'spiritual'. It covers issues that are sometimes simply called 'personal development', and issues that belong to the domain of psychological understanding, but relates these to the deepest values and aspirations of the human spirit.

By now, the question of the importance of the spiritual dimension in edu-cation should be clear enough. It helps to restore the balance in a curriculum whose primary aim is to develop rational/scientific knowledge and under-standing, in schools which are managed increasingly on economic/industrial principles and in leisure time dominated by materialism and consumerism. Ted Hughes (1989) points out that 'a person's own inner world cannot fold up its spiritual wings, shut down all its tuned circuits, and become a mechanical business of nuts and bolts, just because a political or intellectual ideology requires it to' (p. 170). There is a danger that a despiritualized education might seek to do this, to break down children's natural sensitivity to the inner world and imprison them in an impoverished, non-human materialism. John Hull (1996) pictures this danger graphically as the triumph of Mammon as the 'omnipresent and omnipotent creator of human destiny' (p. 40). The education of the human spirit is precisely what is needed to help children to avoid the passive acceptance of the sovereignty of Mammon and to help them to recap-ture their imagination, perception and delight and grow towards autonomy and integrity.

This chapter is concerned with the relationship between three concepts: spirituality, education and the arts. Having discussed the relationship between the first two in the present section, I now want to turn to the relationship between spirituality and the arts and then in the final section look at all three concepts together.

Spirituality and the Arts

In this section I shall argue that the arts 'tap into deep emotional and spiritual currents in human consciousness' (Robinson, 1995, pp. 5–6; cf. Hargreaves, 1983). The arts are vital to spiritual growth and development because they give people a way of expressing their spirituality; and conversely, spirituality is vital to the arts because without it the arts may become a matter of convention or imitation. In a sense, we may say that it is spirituality that breathes life into a work of art. For if we understand the arts to be concerned with the striving for something beyond ourselves, the urge to create and express oneself, the draw-ing on inner resources, the exercise of the imagination and the expression of awe and wonder, then all of these belong to the domain of the human spirit. Langer (1957) provides us with a definition of the arts which clearly encompasses these dimensions:

> Art is . . . the creation of expressive forms — visually, audibly, or even imaginatively perceivable forms — that set forth the nature of human feeling. (p. 111)

I do not wish in this chapter to initiate any discussion about the autonomy of the individual arts or their relationships with each other, which, as Langer (*ibid.*, p. 112) points out, are much more than the possession of some common features or equivalent elements. All that need concern us here is that the various arts — literature, painting, music, drama, dance, poetry and sculpture — have this particular feature in common, that they are concerned with spiritual aspects of life such as creation and the representation of feeling.

Nor is this spiritual dimension part only of the activity of the artist; it is also part of the appreciation of art. Indeed, without it there is a danger that the appreciation of art may become part of the cult of Mammon, in which art is evaluated in terms of its monetary value and the true appreciation of art is replaced by the desire to *possess* an item valued by others, to attend a fashionable performance, to be praised for one's artistic understanding. True appreciation of art, on the other hand, may involve a complex spiritual interaction between the artist and the audience, as Langer indicates:

> In watching a dance, you do not see what is physically before you — people running around or twisting their bodies; what you see is a display of interacting forces, by which the dance seems to be lifted, driven, drawn, closed or attenuated, whether it be solo or choric, whirling like the end of a dervish dance, or slow, centered, and single in its motion. One human body may put the whole play of mysterious forces before you. But these powers, these forces that seem to operate in the dance, are not the physical forces of the dancer's muscles, which actually cause the movements taking place. The forces we seem to perceive most directly and convincingly are created for our perception. (*ibid.*, p. 5)

This is not the place to enter into the debate about the distinction between the aesthetic and the artistic, other than to mention Best's claim that artistic appreciation involves the ability to discuss different interpretations and justify what one values in a work, whereas aesthetic appreciation is more of an instinctive response to something one finds beautiful (Best, 1996, pp. 80–1). Both are related to the spiritual dimension, but the aesthetic more obviously so. Of course, one may have an aesthetic response to many things, not just to works of art: daffodils, a rainbow or a skylark will do, or even a colourful group of water-snakes, as in Coleridge's *Ancient Mariner*:

Within the shadow of the ship
I watched their rich attire:
Blue, glossy green, and velvet black
They coiled and swam; and every track
Was a flash of golden fire.

O happy living things! No tongue
Their beauty might declare:
A spring of love gushed from my heart,
And I blessed them unaware:
Sure my kind saint took pity on me,
And I blessed them unaware.

The selfsame moment I could pray;
And from my neck so free
The albatross fell off, and sank
Like lead into the sea.

What is interesting here is the clear link between the Mariner's aesthetic response to the water-snakes and his spiritual regeneration (cf. Ross, 1982, pp. 79–80). His inner response to their beauty leads to an upsurge of love for creatures outside himself, and this is all that is needed to break his spiritual bondage. Ross develops this as a metaphor for aesthetic education, which he suggests 'seeks to bring the child in to loving relationship with the world sensuously perceived, to provoke experiences of rapture and joy through such encounters and to build the child's self-esteem as a creative and unique human being' (ibid., p. 81). Aesthetic education in this sense clearly has much in common with what I have called the education of the human spirit.

Even in its older, narrower, religious sense, spirituality has highly important links with the arts. As Carr (1995) points out, 'in a very significant sense religion and art speak a common language', since both are more likely to use the 'spiritual language' of symbols, myths, metaphors, parables and analogies rather than the more literal/rational language used in science and logic (p. 95). Art forms such as icons, calligraphy, sculpture, stained glass, mosaics, architecture and religious painting, dance and music may provide an important vehicle for developing an understanding of religious ideas, beliefs and concepts, and for believers such art forms may be an outward expression of inner conviction or of deep religious truth. Conversely, creative artists have often found inspiration in religion. At the beginning of *Paradise Lost* Milton invokes the inspiration of the Holy Spirit in just the same way that classical poets had invoked the Muse. Abdu'l Baha expresses a widely held belief that the arts are inherently religious when he says that 'all art is the gift of the Holy Spirit' and that artistic talents 'are fulfilling their highest purpose when showing forth the praise of God'. The other side of this link between spirituality in its narrower, religious sense and the arts must not be forgotten, however, as Watson (1993, pp. 96–8) warns us: religion has not only inspired some of the finest artistic creations in the world, but it has also given rise to much that is banal, senti-mental and superficial. It is also worth noting that many religions have an ambivalent attitude to art, seen, for example, in Puritan opposition to the theatre and to the ornate decoration of places of worship, and in Muslim opposition to representational art and certain kinds of music (cf. Halstead, 1994a).

Although Fuller (1990) speaks disparagingly of the modern tendency to talk about the 'spiritual' or the 'transcendent' in connection with art rather than the religious, it is clear that spirituality in the sense in which I have defined it in this chapter has a great deal in common with the arts. Let me list some of the parallels.

(a)　The arts, like spirituality, are concerned with the inner life. To start with, the artist must draw on her own inner resources, including a sense of self, a set of emotions, certain qualities of character. Then she must strive to understand the inner life and rhythms of her subject and form. Kandinsky (1970) reserves the highest praise for composers like Schönberg and painters like Cézanne who 'search for spiritual harmony' and have 'the gift of divining the inner life in everything' (p. 17). But the *appreciation* of the arts also involves the inner life. Michael Tippett (1989) suggests that all appreciation of art involves 'escape into the true inner world of feelings' (p. 44). In *The Merchant of Venice*, Lorenzo suggests that the human spirit is dulled by the absence of music within a person or the ability to respond to music:

> The man that hath no music in himself,
> Nor is not moved with concord of sweet sounds,
> Is fit for treasons, stratagems and spoils;
> The motions of his spirit are dull as night,
> And his affections dark as Erebus:
> Let no such man be trusted.　*(Act V, Scene 1)*

(b)　This concern with the inner life is balanced by the externalizing activities of self-expression and creativity. Priestley (1985) suggests that people grow spiritually by measuring their own inwardness 'against the expressed experience of others' (p. 118), and the arts are one of the most important ways of giving expression to this experi-ence. To quote Kandinsky (1970) again, 'the artist must have some-thing to say, for mastery over form is not his goal, but rather the adapting of form to its inner meaning' (p. 54). Artistic creativity on this view has nothing to do with assertive inventiveness, but is more like 'adoring humility before the givenness of both matter and mean-ing' (Watson, 1993, p. 99).

(c)　Like spirituality, the arts are centrally concerned with feelings and the emotions; at least, they are concerned with formulating 'images of feeling' (Langer, 1957, p. 25), and this formulation may involve reason, calculation and purposeful planning, though the final impact may involve only feeling. The arts may inspire awe and wonder, joy and delight, but may also force us to respond to the pain and suffering in the world, and all of these may be seen as elements in spiritual growth.

(d) The arts have the capacity to raise a person above the level of the mundane, to express human longings, to develop the imagination, to encourage reflection on the most profound human experiences, to search for meaning and truth, to link the 'sensuously immediate with the spiritually infinite' (Ross, 1982, p. 82).

Spirituality and Primary Arts Education

It is sometimes suggested that children have a natural spiritual disposition which schools can either develop or neglect. From what has been said already, the contribution that the arts can make towards children's spiritual development is very clear: education in the arts can contribute to the education of the emotions; it can encourage children to draw on their own inner resources and develop their own individuality and personal integrity; it can encourage imagination, self-expression and creativity; it can be a means by which 'they reconstruct and assimilate the experiences they have had' (Barnes, 1987, p. 1); and it can challenge children's attitudes and values and encourage them to aspire to something beyond their present limited world view. But these goals for education, important though they are, are not always given sufficient prominence in schools. All too often in the past the values relating to the education of the human spirit have been left in the domain of the hidden curriculum, so that it is chancy whether children pick them up at all, let alone in an ordered and coherent way.

What is needed is not so much a new range of activities within the primary arts curriculum, as a raising to the consciousness of the primary teacher of the possibilities for developing the fundamental human characteristics and capacities that I have called the human spirit, so that existing activities can be approached in a new light. In order to explore how good practice in arts education can develop the human spirit, and how an understanding of the spiritual dimension can enrich arts education, let us look at one or two specific examples. All of them are drawn from *The Arts 5–16: Practice and Innovation* (Arts in Schools Project Team, 1990), which is interesting because although it makes no direct reference to the spiritual dimension in education it does nonetheless describe several classroom activities rich in potential in this area.

The first example (pp. 25–6) involves the activities of a year 1 class. A series of learning experiences through touch is described, starting in snowplay in early spring and leading through to more arts-specific activities including weaving, braid-making, collage and the making of cardboard box sculptures in the summer term. Although the 'intended learning' of this project is listed under such headings as 'manipulative skills' (cutting, carving, shaping, stretching, bending, and so on) and 'conceptual learning' (light and shade, texture and colour, rough and smooth, etc), and the 'actual learning' is described in terms of 'development of appropriate language' and 'learning to distinguish concepts of contrast . . . (and) between two- and three-dimensional shapes', it is clear that other, unacknowledged kinds of learning are going on as well. There is wonder at the melting of the snowflakes and the shape and texture of the shells; imagination and creativity are being developed through the various planned activities; the children are feeling, exploring, discovering, growing and developing their own individuality in the process. The words quoted earlier about linking the 'sensuously immediate with the spiritually infinite' seem particularly appropriate here.

The second example (pp. 23–4 and 33–4) involves the work of a dance teacher with a county-wide brief whose aims were to challenge boys' stereotypical attitudes to dance by providing opportunities for them to watch and work with male dancers and thus to open up larger issues such as body image, gender and racial stereotyping and different cultural values. Yet behind these overt social and cultural aims was a belief the boys' spiritual development was being impoverished because of their failure to recognize dance as 'physically and psychologically emancipating', with the potential to release 'a vast range of dynamic expression associated with common experience across the sexual divide'.

The third example (pp. 41–2) focuses on a sequence of music lessons planned by a non-specialist first school teacher for a group of 'less able children'. She deliberately built in personal and social as well as artistic criteria into her aims and objectives: 'enjoyment', 'developing self-confidence' and 'working cooperatively as members of a group' were all mentioned as well as developing musical awareness and ability. What she found was that the two sets of aims were mutually reinforcing, so that as the children's confidence and security in the group increased, so did their interest and involvement in the actual music. Others have reported how music can contribute to the early awareness of self and to emotional development in children with special educational needs. Brown (1991), for example, writes that

> Even those children who are not articulate may have a light in their eyes or an expression on their faces; they may alter their posture or the position of their hands, and show many other signs of pleasure, dislike, excitement or joy. (p. 40)

Conclusion

I have argued in this chapter that the arts provide an important way of expressing and developing our spiritual natures as humans, and that paying attention to the spiritual dimension of life enriches our understanding of what education in the arts can achieve. Of course, I do not wish to deny other functions of education in the arts. Indeed, the arts are particularly well placed to serve the interests of all five dimensions of education mentioned in the 1988 Education Act — the spiritual, the moral, the cultural, the mental and the physical. Nor do I wish to suggest that other subjects, such as science and mathematics, have nothing to contribute to the development of emotional responses and the creative imagination or to a growing sense of individuality or personal integrity. The core of my argument has been that the human spirit does not thrive unless nurtured, and that if we want to avoid a dreary, soulless, robot-like existence in the future, then we must nurture it in our children. To end on a prophetic note: I am not alone in sensing a deep spiritual hunger in the world today, especially among many children and young people (cf. Taylor, 1994); in the arts we have the means to satisfy this hunger, and we neglect to do so at our peril.

Bibliography

ARTS IN SCHOOLS PROJECT TEAM (1990) *The Arts 5–16: Practice and Innovation*, Harlow, Oliver and Boyd.

BARNES, R. (1987) *Teaching Art to Young Children 4–9*, London, Allen and Unwin.

BEST, D. (1996) 'Values in the arts' in HALSTEAD, J.M. and TAYLOR, M.J. (Eds) *Values in Education and Education in Values*, London, Falmer Press.

BRADFORD INSPECTION and CULTURAL SERVICES (1990) *The Spiritual Area of Experience: A Framework for Development*, Bradford, Bradford Education.

BROWN, E. (1991) 'The role of music in religious education for pupils with special educational needs' in SHAP WORKING PARTY (Ed) *World Religions in Education 1991–1992: Religious Education and the Creative Arts*, Cambridge, Hobsons.

CARR, D. (1995) 'Towards a distinctive conception of spiritual education', *Oxford Review of Education*, **21**, 1, pp. 83–98.

DES (1985) *The Curriculum from 5 to 16: Curriculum Matters 2 — an HMI Series*, London, HMSO.

FULLER, P. (1990) *Images of God: The Consolations of Lost Illusions*, London, Hogarth Press.

HALLIS (1995) 'Provision of the spiritual', *SPES: a Magazine for the Study of Spiritual, Moral and Cultural Values in Education*, **2**, pp. 6–7.

HALSTEAD, J.M. (1992) 'The final frontier', *The Times Educational Supplement Special Report on Religious Education*, 18 December.

HALSTEAD, J.M. (1994a) 'Muslim attitudes to music in schools', *British Journal of Music Education*, **11**, 2, pp. 143–56.

HALSTEAD, J.M. (1994b) 'Moral and spiritual education in Russia', *Cambridge Journal of Education*, **24**, 3, pp. 423–38.

HARGREAVES, D.H. (1983) 'Dr Brunel and Mr Dunning: Reflections on aesthetic knowing' in Ross, M. (Ed) *The Arts as a Way of Knowing*, Oxford, Pergamon Press.

HERTFORDSHIRE EDUCATION SERVICES (1993) *Spiritual and Moral Development: Guidance for Schools*, Wheathampstead, Hertfordshire Education Services Religious Education Centre.

HUGHES, T. (1989) 'Myth and education' in ABBS, P. (Ed) *The Symbolic Order: A Contemporary Reader on the Arts Debate*, London, Falmer Press.

HULL, J.M. (1993) 'In the body or out of the boyd...? Spirituality or materiality', a keynote address to the National Conference on Moral and Spiritual Education, University of Plymouth, September.

HULL, J.M. (1996) 'The ambiguity of spiritual values' in HALSTEAD, J.M. and TAYLOR, M.J. (Eds) *Values in Education and Education in Values*, London, Falmer Press.

KANDINSKY, W. (1970) *Concerning the Spiritual in Art* (originally published in 1911 as *Über das Geistige in der Kunst*), New York, Dover Publications.

LANGER, S.K. (1957) *Problems of Art: The Philosophical Lectures*, New York, Charles Scribner's Sons.

MICHAUD, C. (1994) 'Société pluraliste et diversité des experiences spirituelles chez les jeunes adultes', *The Journal of Educational Thought*, **28**, 1, pp. 34–58.

MINISTRY OF EDUCATION (1963) *Half our Future (The Newsom Report)*, London, HMSO.

MINNEY, R. (1991) 'What is spirituality in an educational context?' *British Journal of Educational Studies*, **39**, 4, pp. 386–97.

OFSTED (1994) *Spiritual, Moral, Social and Cultural Development: An OFSTED Discussion Paper*, London, OFSTED.

PATTEN, J. (1992) 'Don't sell pupils short', *The Tablet*, 10 October, pp. 1256–7.

PRIESTLEY, J.G. (1985) 'Towards finding the hidden curriculum: A consideration of the spiritual dimension of experience in curriculum planning', *British Journal of Religious Education*, **7**, 3, pp. 112–9.

ROBINSON, K. (1995) 'Children, society and the arts', *Children and Society*, **9**, 4, pp. 5–14.

ROSS, M. (1982) 'Knowing face to face: Towards mature aesthetic encountering' in ROSS, M. (Ed) *The Development of Aesthetic Experience*, Oxford, Pergamon Press.

SCAA (1995) *Spiritual and Moral Development SCAA Discussion Papers No 3*, London, SCAA.

STARKINGS, D. (1993) 'The landscape of spirituality' in STARKINGS, D. (Ed) *Religion and the Arts in Education: Dimensions of Spirituality*, Sevenoaks, Hodder and Stoughton.

TAYLOR, E. (1994) 'Desperately seeking spirituality', *Psychology Today*, 27, 6, pp. 54–68.

TIPPETT, M. (1989) 'Art, judgment and belief: Towards the condition of music' in ABBS, P. (Ed) *The Symbolic Order: A Contemporary Reader on the Arts Debate*, London, Falmer Press.

WATSON, B. (1993) 'The arts as a dimension of religion' in STARKINGS, D. (Ed) *Religion and the Arts in Education: Dimensions of Spirituality*, Sevenoaks, Hodder and Stoughton.

8 Using the Arts to Explore Issues of Loss, Death and Bereavement

Valerie Clark

To see education only as a preparation for something that happens later, risks overlooking the needs and opportunities of the moment. Children do not hatch into adults after a secluded incubation at school. They are living their lives now. Helping them towards an independent and worthwhile life in the adult world of the future presupposes helping them to make sense of and deal with the experiences which they suffer and enjoy in the present. (Gulbenkian Report, 1982, p. 4)

Needs and Opportunities of the Moment

Education must, of necessity, be both present and future focused since it has to attend to the current experiences of pupils while also preparing them for 'the opportunities, responsibilities and experiences of adult life' (Education Reform Act, 1988, 2b). While schools may be able to prepare pupils reasonably adequately for the social transition into adult roles of employee, citizen and parent, events such as the death of a loved one are psychological and emotional changes for which people are never really prepared, whatever their age. Bereavement is an inevitable and universal experience to which our relationships and friendships expose us and can occur, without warning, at any time in life as the death of another person usually cannot be planned or anticipated. In fact, the term 'bereavement' indicates survivorship status because it refers to the state of a person who has lost someone significant by death.

When children experience such an event, particularly the death of a parent or sibling, it may be difficult for them to cope with their emotions and to make sense of what has happened. At such a time some pupils may find the atmosphere and routine of school life provides a refuge from the unsettled and uncertain situation of home but, for others, school may be too demanding in terms of attendance, work and concentration.

I suggest that in a sense, the grieving period never ends but, with the passing of time, some of the earlier sharp grief abates. After about two years the pain has probably lessened as the death is reality-tested by a range of anniversaries such as birthdays of the bereaved and deceased, the death itself, national and religious holidays and other family get-togethers.

The growth and acceptance of bereavement counselling in Britain and elsewhere seems to have encouraged a recognition of the need to talk about the event — to 'give sorrow words' in order to keep the 'o'erfraught heart' from breaking (Shakespeare, *Macbeth*, Act IV, Scene 3). Not only words, whether spoken or written, but other forms of self-expression such as painting and drawing can give voice or form to the many losses everyone experiences in life as relationships, situations and expectations change (Viorst, 1986).

Within the school curriculum, most arts subjects can develop attitudes and skills that may be helpful at various stages in the grieving process since they are believed to encourage:

- self-expression, self-understanding and self-awareness;
- imagination, perception and recall;
- mutual cooperation and respect for other people's viewpoints;
- empathic links with and appreciation of nature, the world and/or the cosmos.
  (Ross, 1980; Taylor and Andrews, 1991; National Curriculum Council, 1990)

A common strand in Attainment Target 1 in *Art In the National Curriculum* (1992) is to record what has been seen, imagined or remembered and such recording can allow pupils to legitimately relive and explore their experiences of bereavement and loss.

Bereavement in the Primary School Years

The death of a pet or grandparent may be common during the primary school years but an awareness of such events seems particularly heightened by the early teens. For example, when I asked them to do so, sixty-six 11–12-year-olds recorded 151 deaths including sixty-eight grandparents, fifty pets, sixteen friends, seven siblings and one parent. Twenty-six of the sixty-six pupils re-membered deaths when they were aged 10, twenty-one when they were aged 9, and twelve when they were aged 5 (Clark, 1996).

In figure 8.1 below I suggest that the deaths of elderly people (for example, grandparents) may not be so significant to primary school pupils because such deaths are usually anticipated and, unless certain circumstances prevail (as suggested in figure 8.2), they seem timely and do not challenge the belief that older things die first. Similarly, the death of distant family members and non-family members is usually less distressing because these people are not so well known to young children.

Figure 8.1: Deaths that are usually not significant

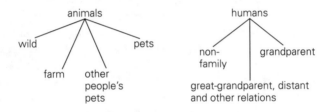

Figure 8.2: Deaths that may be significant depending on circumstances

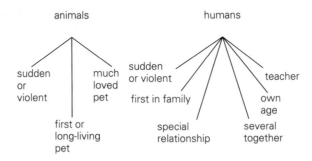

However, sudden or violent death (perhaps by murder, suicide or accident) and the death of a peer usually seem important or significant because of their untimeliness. People with whom one has a special relationship (whether family or not) are often greatly missed and a teacher's death may be particularly distressing for children because of the close or regular nature of the relationship. The first death in a family may be a shock and the clustering of several together often seems significant also. In fact, five of the six factors specific to human death in figure 8.2 were present when sixteen pupils and a teacher died at Dunblane Primary School in March 1996 and the national response to those deaths (for example, *The Independent*, 18 March) probably reflected the impact of such confounding.

Deaths that are usually significant, whatever one's age, are those of parents (Abrams, 1992; McLoughlin, 1994) or siblings (SIBBS) and, for parents, the death of a child is often overwhelming (The Compassionate Friends). However, improved medical and health care can now enable many people to live longer and to die at an age that few reached in previous generations. Since many adults do not encounter a first significant bereavement until they are in their thirties or forties, some teachers will not have experienced the sort of bereavement that a pupil is currently facing. Whatever their age, though, all bereaved people need time to respond to changed personal circumstances. This may mean that pupils need to take time out from studying or to do so less intensively and that teachers have to resolve a conflict between the professional role of educator and the personal need to grieve.

Ephemeral and Concrete Art Forms: Reflections of Living and Dying

Despite — or perhaps because of — the paradox of humanity's awareness of both its uniqueness within the created world and also its inevitable demise (Becker, 1973), a common human feature seems to be the need to produce symbolic forms of immortality (Lifton and Olson, 1974) which, while acknowledging that death is final, give people a sense of connection with the future beyond their present individual lives. These forms include having a sense of continuity through children and family; creating and influencing (teaching, writing, inventing, constructing); uniting with nature (enjoying and caring for it while alive and returning to it, reconstituted, when dead); and transcending the present moment or living it to the full (for example, through music or physical activity).

Some people may develop their imaginative capacities as compensation for the absence of intimate relationships with family members since, by creating a poem, story or other work of art which has a concrete presence in the world, a lost unity may be restored or a new unity found within oneself. Thus the gap between the external world of reality and an individual's inner world is bridged (Storr, 1989). As creative people are often used to or prefer solitude in order to work, bereaved children may have an advantage in having had to cope with being left alone, either physically or psychologically, at significant times in their lives. Writing, painting or shaping a product can be a practical way of overcoming feelings of helplessness — which a bereavement in childhood may engender — or of overcoming anger at feeling abandoned.

It may be that the greater the disharmony within — whether caused by bereavement or some other form of stress — 'the sharper the spur to seek harmony, or, if one has the gifts, to *create* harmony' (*ibid.*, p. 132). For example, Sylvia Plath had such abilities and used them to describe her inner world and, apparently, to predict her own suicide. She was a child prodigy and published her first poem when she was 8, a year before her father died. Although an outstanding student, she attempted suicide at 19/20 and again at 29/30 when married with two children and in *Daddy* (1962) she seems to explain why.

> I was ten when they buried you.
> At twenty I tried to die
> And get back, back, back to you.
> I thought even the bones would do.

While I am not advocating the exploration of suicidal thoughts with children, I contend that many forms of literature and visual art contain expressions and explorations of grief, shock and sorrow which are natural human responses to bereavement and loss. For example Pablo Picasso's *Guernica* probably depicts the events of an earthquake he experienced in Malaga when aged 3 (Miller,

1991, p. 12); *A woman entrusts herself to death* may show how Kathe Kollwitz interpreted her mother's response to the deaths of three of her children, Kathe's siblings, when she was growing up (*ibid.*, pp. 30–1); William Cowper's *On the receipt of my mother's picture out of Norfolk* recaptures childhood memories of his mother who died when he was 6 (Storr, 1989, p. 134); and Charlotte Bronte's *Jane Eyre* describes the deaths of her sisters at boarding school when she was 9 (Nestor, 1987).

It is interesting to note that one strand in Attainment Target 2 in art is for pupils to apply knowledge of the work of other artists to their own. I suggest that such knowledge could include an understanding of the personal and emotional reasons for the artist's choice of subject as well as of the media and methods used.

Creative, Performing, Verbal and Contemplative Arts

A painting, drawing, sculpture, poem, play, story, piece of craft work or writing can serve two purposes. As a creative process, it enables the bereaved person to emotionally and cognitively relive memories, feelings and hopes during its physical creation and, as a finished product or event, it can stand as a memorial to the relationship the bereaved person had with the deceased. Rubin (1984), an art therapist, eloquently describes this dual purpose when, after a friend died when she was 17, she felt compelled to paint something.

> The painting was not of my friend, but of someone playing the piano, making music in dark reds, purples, and blacks. It was a cry, a scream caught and tamed. It was a new object in the world, perhaps a replacement for the person who was gone, as well as a mature, tangible testament. The doing of it afforded tremendous relief. It did not take away the hurt and the ache, but it did help in releasing some of the rage and in giving form to the confused feelings which threatened to overwhelm me. (p. 10)

Similarly, Alfred Tennyson began writing *In Memoriam* a few days after the death of his friend Hallam and continued to work on the poem for nearly seventeen years (Storr, 1989). Although not originally intended for publication, it stands as a tribute to their friendship and shows how a poet used his talent to deal with his grieving. In a different way Patricia Beer's *Beach Party* (1993) captures the insight — recognized in adulthood — that only a week after their mother's death 'we found we could still play' as well as her awareness that:

> All afternoon
> Pretending to be sad which they understood,
> I watched the empty sand
> On the other side of me.

In what follows, I shall discuss the different approaches offered by four arts areas — creative, performing, verbal and contemplative — when thinking about and depicting loss and bereavement issues.

The so-called creative arts (painting, drawing, sculpting, craft and design) usually involve making a product. Such 'making' may involve representing or expressing in concrete or semi-concrete form one's own inner world; gaining control of or manipulating substances and media; and breaking, reworking or destroying the whole product or parts of it — which may also stand as a substitute for something else. Such activities can have great therapeutic value in allowing the legitimate expression of (for example) anger, confusion, sorrow and fear as necessary components of the creative and grieving process.

As well as the therapeutic satisfaction of creating such products, their concrete or semi-concrete form also enables them to endure. This outcome may also indicate humanity's desire to transcend its limits, to create a lasting product, and to impose order on the apparently chaotic world in which we live.

The performing arts (dance, music, drama) are a form of interpretation. They are also a useful and metaphorical means of enabling people to rework the past, to explore alternatives, to risk making mistakes, and to release tension. Moreno (1972) recognized these qualities when he developed psychodrama as a therapeutic means of exploring real or symbolic problems of importance to an individual or a group.

In a similar way, the often tedious process of rehearsing in non-therapeutic and classroom drama situations enables 'errors' to be made and 'corrected', ideas to be shared and explored and a sense of group cooperation and identity to develop. Long before this art form (which is both verbal and performing) was subsumed by the National Curriculum within English, Heathcote (1972) underlined the value of drama, explaining that, if a teacher is 'concerned with maturity rather than factual knowledge', his or her main way of teaching

> is in the provision of situations which challenge the energies, the intelligence and the efforts of the children in his [sic] class. It is as a releaser of energy that drama is valuable to him. (p. 157)

Drama is concerned with exploring what people say, think and do when they are emotionally involved in compelling events. Therapeutically, its main value is for participants who 'live through' the process of creating and resolving a dilemma and, each time they speak or move, re-live what those interactions mean for them. Such 'living through' may be further enhanced by the response of an audience to what it sees and hears the performers doing.

Drama and dance, in particular, can enable the exploration of personal awareness and discernment through exploration of the senses, emotions and feelings, memory, imagination, and interaction with other people. Although currently located within National Curriculum Physical Education, dance possesses qualities that encourage creative individuality. It uses no language and asks the body to move in unconventional ways — perhaps by moving to a rhythm and suggesting or becoming other human or non-human forms by a change of stance and shape. As well as responding to the rhythm, volume or images of music (if used), dance often involves making decisions about the proximity of other people and how to respond to their movements and gestures. Both drama and dance offer a unique opportunity for unspoken physical interaction which may be beneficial in developing trust and empathy.

Although the composition of a piece of music may be the work of an individual, its performance involves a high degree of cooperation from a group. Participating in this kind of group activity might also be of benefit for bereaved pupils since they find, in a symbolic way, that their contribution to the whole sound picture is necessary and that they have a small part to play in a greater whole. Such an insight may have metaphorical meaning for seeing how each individual life also 'fits' into a larger whole, whether or not this 'fit' is ongoingly apparent. Drama productions, also, have the same element of dependency and involvement and rehearsals always proceed on the assumption that no-one will be ill 'on the night' because this might mean that the production cannot take place. Team work is essential backstage, too, and many pupils enjoy the sense of importance and belonging that such activities entail as the rest of the cast rely upon them simply 'to be there' doing their job.

Play scripts and dance and music scores are tangible but each performance given from them is ephemeral and specific to that moment in time and, like the life of a person and the events of life itself, cannot really be repeated. This is the quintessential element of a performance that is often hard to explain. Even if the performance does not go as planned — despite many hours of rehearsal — for the period of time the play, concert or show is 'running' it is 'alive', with a life and a mystery of its own that transcends the individual contributions made by those taking part. People work together on a task that is bigger than and beyond themselves, often displaying selflessness and compassion as they do so, and using such qualities or being the focus of them can empower the grieving process as a pupil's sense of importance and worth are validated.

The verbal arts (writing prose, poetry, drama) which are closely related to the performing arts are expressive forms using language to explore feelings and emotions, however inadequately. Although it may be undeniable that language is the means whereby social reality is constructed (Berger and Luckman, 1967), for most people, particularly children, the world that language describes *is* the reality within which they live. By naming or describing a feeling, situation or belief, and thus putting into words ideas that were hitherto unexpressed, people are often helped to better understand themselves and their world — and, if necessary, to find ways to change it. In fact *English in the National Curriculum* (HMSO, 1990, p. 24) suggests that verbal forms such as prose, poetry and drama enable pupils to:

- express and justify feelings, opinions and viewpoints with increasing sophistication;

- recount events and narrate stories;
- present ideas, experiences and understanding in a widening range of contexts across the curriculum.

The contemplative arts (reading, observing, watching, listening) are forms of reflection which may seem passive but can be a necessary means of with-drawal into and/or exploration of the ideas and expressions of others. Since art forms are neither right nor wrong but a representation of a particular point of view or way of seeing life, audiences, readers, viewers and spectators may respond to these forms as they wish and, for some people, the artist's view may resound with their own and bring insight and relief.

In line with this recognition that art forms such as stories can validate the experiences of their readers, many teachers include in class libraries fiction and non-fiction which recount some of the sorrows of children's lives such as bullying, broken friendships, bereavement, illness, parental arguments, separ-ation and divorce as a form of 'bibliotherapy' (Bernstein, 1983; Oberstein and VanHorn, 1988). Fictional images can 'reduce the individual's sense of isola-tion and open the mind to previously considered ideas and behaviours' while dialogue (and drawing) can give vision and focus to deeply felt emotions and concerns (Bertman, 1979, p. 148). Some examples which explore death and bereavement for primary pupils include: *Let's Talk About Death And Dying* (Sanders, 1990), *A Taste Of Blackberries* (Smith, 1973) and *Badger's Parting Gifts* (Varley, 1985) (see also *Letterbox Library* and reading lists provided by 'Cruse' and 'The Compassionate Friends': addresses at end of this chapter).

Opportunities and Problems when Using these Art Forms

The growing use of the arts in a range of therapeutic situations (Anderson, 1977; Bunt, 1994; Jennings, 1987) may suggest that such forms are best left to professionals in those fields or that if they are used by teachers, they should not use them with young children. I shall explore some of these assumptions below.

It is probably true that the creative arts are the most widely used form of self-exploration among therapists and counsellors who work with children suddenly or violently bereaved of a parent (Cooley, 1992; Black and Kaplan, 1993) and/or who display emotional and behavioural problems (Pennells and Smith, 1995). There is value in drawing the deceased in a variety of moods and activities (Cooley) or the moment of death (Black) since ambivalent emotions can be acknowledged and facts about the death communicated, such as what the child saw or knows.

In ordinary classroom situations, however, children may also use draw-ings to explore the recent death of a relative (Gulliver, 1997) pet (Kellman, 1995), ideas of an afterlife (Kellman) or the image they have of themselves now that they are bereaved (Bowes, 1990). Teachers should be aware of this need and learn to accept such drawings as attempts by their pupils to relocate the deceased or to explore and resolve emotions. Pupils may only need to draw and colour such images in order to tell others that the events portrayed actually happened. There may be no need for teachers to 'counsel' pupils, merely to acknowledge what is being communicated, although both trainee and experienced teachers will have to learn how best to respond to such apparently unexpected material.

The performing arts, particularly drama, can serve as a vivid form of reenactment. As a teacher of drama I have witnessed the power of improvisation to recreate an angry or troubling scenario to which participants must immediately and directly respond by reliving or subtly changing the outcome, and I have also used the more structured format of scripts to explore human responses to loss and death. Although it is obviously inappropriate to attempt psychodrama with young pupils, it is safe to explore and discuss ways of resolving a problem in order to show how differently people cope. Because drama is undoable and did not really happen, it is a safe way of exploring real life issues.

Casdagli *et al.* (1992) explain that the Neti Neti Theatre Company developed the idea for their play *Grief* after devising *Only Playing, Miss* in which they depict a bully who continues to talk about his mother as if she were still alive. Casdagli *et al.* say that an educational consultant and therapist 'confirmed for us that there was a definite link between "disruptive behaviour" and unresolved grief' (p. 1) and such an awareness may enable teachers to understand the feelings underlying a variety of anti-social and troublesome behaviour exhibited by some of their pupils.

Lucie-Smith (1964) explores the links between bereavement and bullying in *The Lesson*, this time from the victim's viewpoint — and possibly from personal experience. The bullied child expects a reprieve from attack, however brief, after his father's death since he knows that even bullies grudgingly abide by such a code of conduct at such a time.

> 'Your father's gone,' my bald headmaster said.
> His shiny dome and brown tobacco jar
> Splintered at once in tears. It wasn't grief.
> I cried for knowledge which was bitterer
> Than any grief. For there and then I knew
> That grief has uses — that a father dead
> Could bind the bully's fist a week or two;
> And then I cried for shame, then for relief.

When *Grief* went on tour, schools were asked to provide a staffed 'safe' room to which pupils could go if they preferred not to watch because of their own bereavements. Casdagli describes how, despite reading the preliminary material, one teacher 'had not made the connection' between the story of their play

and the recent identical experience of one of her pupils until that pupil walked
out of the performance. Somewhat troubled, the teacher said:

> I could kick myself. X is a truant. This is her first day back in school
> for weeks, and we brought her to see the play, but her twin brother
> was killed in a motorbike accident some months ago. I didn't think.
> (Casdagli *et al.*, 1992, p. 9)

Such an example underlines the need for teachers to carefully read descriptions of classroom materials and books they provide for their pupils — whether
or not for use as direct bibliotherapy — in order to assess their likely impact.
However, such assessing requires an accurate, up-to-date knowledge of
pupils' personal circumstances that is not always possible. In talking about a
particular book, teachers also need to be skilled in asking questions, capable
of showing empathy and knowledgeable of the developmental levels of their
pupils (Guy, 1993).

Verbal arts often involve telling a story, and stories contain two useful
contradictory elements — distancing and involvement — which enable metaphorical reflection on life's pain and grievances. Distancing is often provided
by 'once upon a time' beginnings and the use of royal, supernatural or animal
characters, while involvement arises from identification with the familiar ideas
and emotional life of such characters. A good story is one which, set at a safe
distance from the everyday life of readers and listeners, encourages them to
empathize with the characters in order to gain insight and experience catharsis
(Ayalon in Gersie, 1991).

Myths, legends and folk tales often provide a convenient 'distance' from
which to think about death and bereavement and the origin of death is commonly explained by myths of forbidden fruit, delayed or garbled messages,
moulting animals, the moon, the banana and overpopulation (Corcos and
Krupka, 1978). For example, among the bushmen of Africa the origin of death
is explained by the story of the moon and hare, and in Melanesia by the story
of the woman who cast her skin like a snake (Gersie, 1991). How people feel
when bereaved is explored in the Icelandic story of Baldr and in the Greek
story of Persephone and Demeter (Jordan, 1993). Such stories can help not
only grieving pupils to realize that their present feelings are natural and universal but also prepare other pupils who have not yet been significantly bereaved for future losses.

The contemplative arts, like the verbal arts, may involve reading texts or
listening to others doing so. As previously stated, this kind of involvement may
seem passive but can involve an evaluation of one's own and other's ideas,
whether or not such evaluations are explicitly expressed. An overlap between
creative and contemplative arts exists in the area of fantasy and, within pastoral care and counselling, there is growing discussion of the possible uses of
this approach. Guided fantasy uses a starting image to enable each individual
to relive and reexamine parts of her or his life while scripted fantasy uses the

same story with all members of a group and allows for individual interpretations (Bowes, 1990).

A combined use of relaxation, drawing and fantasy — perhaps using a sufficiently distancing object such as a tree — may enable pupils to safely express negative emotions by projecting them onto the object. A girl recently bereaved of her father who took part in one of these sessions drew herself as a cocker-spaniel, explaining:

> The animal painting meant a lot to me, as I felt it really expressed my inner feelings — feelings of loneliness, fear and the feeling of being lost in a world that is too big for me, involving things that I feel I can perhaps no longer cope with. (*ibid.*, p. 14)

Although this comment is by a secondary school pupil, such insight may be experienced by younger pupils even if it is not so well expressed. However, Bowes (*ibid.*) expresses caution in using these techniques since the atmosphere of such sessions can become emotional and teachers need to adopt a firm non-interpretative and non-judgmental stance.

The Role of the Arts in Death Education

Some of the value in using drawing, painting, craft and other similar art forms may be that they involve the right brain which governs non-verbal intuitive processes, visual and spatial thinking, emotions and fantasy. In fact art work seems to be a useful medium for accessing emotional material and many art sessions are characterized by silence and concentration 'as if the verbal left-brain processes have been bypassed' (*ibid.*, p. 13). Since there is a tendency in education to stress logical, analytical and verbal skills, any redressing of the balance is helpful, especially if such redressing helps bereaved pupils to come to terms with aspects of life such as loss and death to which there are no easy answers. All religions offer an explanation for death but there can never be any empirical evidence that they are correct and perhaps this is why death — and bereavement experiences too — are often described in poetic and metaphorical terms. At some stage in life everyone asks the impossible-to-answer questions: 'Where did I come from? Why am I here? Why am I going through this experience now? Where will I go to after death?' and, in both concrete and semi-concrete forms, writers, musicians, craftspeople and artists have ongoingly explored some possible answers using movement, space, colour, language, shape, light, sound and silence.

If education is seen as a simultaneous preparation for something that happens later as well as an acknowledgment of what is happening now, the arts can be a powerful means of educating about the complexity of both life and death, living and dying by their various uses of metaphor, distancing, transience and concreteness. Elsewhere (Clark, 1990) I have argued for the introduction of 'death education' into the curriculum in order to:

- inform pupils of facts not currently widespread in society (for example, dispelling myths about dying people's pain);
- help pupils deal with their feelings about their own deaths and the deaths of significant others in their lives;
- make pupils informed consumers of medical and funeral services (for example, discussing ethical and financial decisions before the emotional responses to death affects such decision making);
- help pupils clarify their values on social and ethical issues (for example, considering the use of living organ transplants).

I believe that such initiatives are necessary in order to enable primary pupils — who, in ten years or so, will be deemed adult members of society — to live more effectively. Although we may be educating pupils for changing family relationships, citizenship status and employment situations, there will always be a need for them to cope with experiences of loss and bereavement. As I have already shown, the creative, performing, verbal and contemplative arts offer specific yet common approaches which enable this learning process. I believe that the value of the arts lies in their ability to depict and explore universal human experiences in ways that enable people to recognize that they are capable of facing and working through such life-changing events.

Bibliography

ABRAMS, R. (1992) *When Parents Die*, London, Letts & Co.

Art In The National Curriculum (1992) London, HMSO.

ANDERSON, W. (1977) (Ed) *Therapy And The Arts: Tools Of Consciousness*, New York, Harper Colophon.

AYALON, O. (1991) 'Foreword' in GERSIE, A. *Storymaking In Bereavement*, London, Jessica Kingsley.

BECKER, E. (1973) *The Denial Of Death*, New York, Mcmillan.

BEER, P. (1993) 'Beach party' in *Friend of Heraclitus*, Manchester, Carcanet Press.

BERGER, P. and LUCKMAN, T. (1967) *The Social Construction Of Reality*, New York, Doubleday.

BERNSTEIN, J.E. (1983) *Books To Help Children Cope With Separation And Loss* (2nd edn) New York, Bowker.

BERTMAN, S. (1979) 'The arts: A source of comfort and insight for children who are learning about death' *Omega*, **10**, 2, pp. 147–62.

BLACK, D. and KAPLAN, T. (1993) 'Father kills mother: Post-traumatic stress disorder in the children', *Bereavement Care*, **12**, 1, pp. 9–11.

BOWES, M. (1990) 'Art and fantasy: Theory into practice', *Pastoral Care*, **8**, 2, pp. 10–15.

BUNT, L. (1994) *Music Therapy: An Art Beyond Words*, London, Routledge.

CASDAGLI, P., GOBEY, F. and GRIFFIN, C. (1992) *Grief: The Play, Writings And Workshops*, London, Fulton.

CLARK, V. (1990) 'Death education: An education for life?', *Curriculum*, **12**, 1, pp. 42–52.

CLARK, V. (1996) 'Bereavement and moral and spiritual development: An exploration of the experiences of children and young people', unpublished PhD thesis, University of Plymouth.

THE COMPASSIONATE FRIENDS (undated pamphlet) 'No death so sad', York, The Compassionate Friends.

COOLEY, J. (1992) 'Searching for a way through: An account of bereavement work with a 7-year-old boy', *Bereavement Care*, **11**, 1, pp. 11–13.

CORCOS, A. and KRUPKA, L. (1978) 'How death came to mankind: Myths and legands' in KALISH, R.A. (Ed) *The Final Transition*, New York, Baywood.

Education Reform Act (1988) London, HMSO.

English in the National Curriculum (1990) London, HMSO.

GERSIE, A. (1991) *Storymaking In Bereavement*, London, Jessica Kingsley.

GULBENKIAN REPORT (1982) *The Arts In Schools: Principles, Practices And Provision*, London, Calouste Gulbenkian Foundation.

GULLIVER, J. (1997) 'Beginnings, middles and ends: Whose realities? in HOLT, D. (Ed) *Primary Arts Education: Contemporary Issues*, London, Falmer Press.

GUY, T. (1993) 'Exploratory study of elementary-aged children's conceptions of death through the use of story', *Death Studies*, **17**, 1, pp. 27–54.

HEATHCOTE, D. (1972) 'Drama as challenge' in HODGSON, J. (Ed) *The Uses Of Drama*, London, Eyre Methuen.

The Independent (1996) 'The day a nation fell silent', 18 March, p. 1; 'In every home and workplace, time stands still as a nation grieves for the children of class P1', 18 March, pp. 2–3.

JENNINGS, S. (1987) *Dramatherapy: Theory And Practice For Teachers And Clinicians*, Beckenham, Croom Helm.

JORDAN, M. (1993) *Myths of The World: A Thematic Encyclopedia*, London, Kyle Cathie.

KELLMAN, J. (1995) 'Harvey shows the way: Narrative in children's art', *Art Education*, March, pp. 18–22.

LIFTON, R.J. and OLSON, E. (1974) *Living And Dying*, London, Wildwood.

LUCIE-SMITH, E. (1964) 'The lesson', *Penguin Modern Poets 6*, Harmondsworth, Penguin.

MCLOUGHLIN, J. (1994) *On The Death Of A Parent*, London, Virago.

MILLER, A. (1991) *The Untouched Key: Tracing Childhood Trauma in Creativity and Destructiveness*, London, Virago.

MORENO, J.L. (1972) 'Drama as therapy' in HODGSON, J. (Ed) *The Uses Of Drama*, London, Eyre Methuen.

NCC (1990) *Arts In Schools Project: The Arts 5–16: Practice and Innovation*, London, Oliver & Boyd.

NESTOR, P. (1987) *Charlotte Bronte*, London, Macmillan.

OBERSTEIN, K. and VANHORN, R. (1988) 'Books can help heal: Innovative techniques in bibilotherapy', *Florida Media Quarterly*, **13**, 2, pp. 4–11.

PENNELLS, M. and SMITH, S. (1995) *The Forgotten Mourners*, London, Jessica Kingsley.

PLATH, S. (1962) 'Daddy', *The New Poetry*, Harmondworth, Penguin.

ROSS, M. (1980) 'The arts and personal growth' in ROSS, M. (Ed) *The Arts And Personal Growth*, Oxford, Pergamon Press.

RUBIN, J.A. (1984) *Child Art Therapy* (2nd edn) New York, Van Nostrand Reinhold.

SANDERS, P. (1990) *Let's Talk About: Death And Dying*, London, Aladdin.

SHAKESPEARE, W. (1963) *Macbeth*, New York, Signet.

SIBBS (Support in bereavement for brothers and sisters) *Newsletter* York, The Compassionate Friends.

SMITH, D.B. (1973) *A Taste Of Blackberries*, Harmondsworth, Puffin.

STORR, A. (1989) *Solitude*, London, Collins/Fontana.

TAYLOR, R. and ANDREWS, G. (1991) *The Arts In Primary Education*, London, Falmer Press.

TENNYSON, A. (1974) *In Memorium, Maud and Other Poems*, London, Dent/Everyman.

VARLEY, S. (1985) *Badger's Parting Gifts*, London, Collins.

VIORST. J. (1986) *Necessary Losses: The Loves, Illusions, Dependencies and Impossible Expectations That All Of Us Have To Give Up In Order To Grow*, London, Simon & Schuster.

Groups and Publishers

The Compassionate Friends (self-help group of parents bereaved of a child) 53 North Street, Bristol, BS3 1EN.

Cruse (counselling for all bereaved people) Cruse House, 126 Sheen Road, Richmond, Surrey, TW9 1UR.

Letterbox Library, Unit 2D, Leroy House, 436 Essex Road, London, N1 3QP.

9   Music Technology in the Primary Classroom

Will McBurnie

Introduction

The Working Group for Music in the National Curriculum, set up in 1990 by the Secretary of State for Education and Science, identified the fact that few primary schools used microcomputers for music (DES, 1990, p. 5, para. 2.13). The evidence base for this claim was HMI visits to almost 500 primary schools between 1982 and 1989. The finding was hardly surprising given the infancy of the technology: there has been considerable development in computer hardware and software packages available to schools since that time. Perhaps more surprising is the lack of mention in the HMI evidence of electronic music keyboards in primary schools. These have been available at inexpensive prices since the early-mid 1980s and many children have access to them in their own homes. It is true that, ten years on from the general availability of such music technology, there is still relatively little use of music technology being made in primary schools.

This chapter is for all those concerned with teacher education in music, including teachers themselves involved in teaching music in primary schools, whether or not they currently make use of music technology. It does not concern itself with endless 'tips' on what to do with keyboards, computers or other forms of music technology in the classroom. Rather, it addresses a range of issues that teachers might consider in approaching the use of music technology in music education and should thus be helpful to teachers as they develop their own rationale for the use of music technology. As with the advent of other new technologies, music technology presents opportunities for enhancing the quality of teaching and learning. However, quality will not be achieved without commitment from the teacher for the use of music technology in music education and an understanding on her/his behalf of the opportunities and problems this presents. This is a fundamental issue in the use of music technology in music education.

Some teachers might be attracted to the use of music technology by the 'glamour' of the technology rather than the educational value it might offer. Others may be put off from making any use of music technology in their teaching for a variety of reasons. They might:

— be daunted by the range of music technology available;
— lack technical understanding for the operation of the equipment;
— have little or no understanding of how music technology can contribute to children's music education.

Strategies need to be put in place by teacher educators to deal with each of these points. However, it is the final point that is the key to accessing music technology to enhance the quality of music education. It is important that a teacher's commitment to the use of music technology should come from an understanding of how it can effectively become a part of children's music education; enabling children to work as musicians and to develop their skills and understanding in music.

Underpinning Our Music Teaching

Implicit in this last statement is that teachers have a rationale for their music teaching. Indeed most teachers do have their own rationale which is based upon their understanding and experience of teaching and learning, child development and music. It is healthy for us all to continually reconsider our own rationale: it should be modified in the light of our own learning. I recommend such as Glover and Ward (1993), Mills (1991) and Swanwick (1988 and 1994) as excellent sources for teachers to develop their thinking and understanding about music education. It is important that we evaluate our music teaching in parallel with our thinking about music education.

Although teachers are given a framework for teaching music through the National Curriculum, they need to have an understanding and belief in what they are trying to achieve in music education and why and how they are trying to achieve it. Research by Lawson, Plummeridge and Swanwick (Lawson *et al.*, 1994) indicates that the position of music studies in the primary classroom varies greatly from school to school. They also found that:

> Many teachers referred to the value of musical encounters in terms
> of pupils' intellectual, emotional, spiritual and social development.
> (p. 12)

It is not the place of this chapter to discuss the reasons for the variety of practice in music education in primary classrooms. However, we should take heart from the fact that many teachers, in the research of Lawson *et al.*, had a similar belief in why music is important in the primary classroom. It might seem obvious, but it is something which teachers should hold on to amongst the day-to-day 'routine' of their work.

National Curriculum

With a rationale for teaching music in the primary classroom, we can look to the National Curriculum for music as our framework for guidance. We can then consider the best opportunities open to us to make effective use of music technology in our teaching and our pupils' learning. It is interesting to note that, apart from the reference to technology in the common requirements for Programmes of Study in the National Curriculum, the only reference to IT at Key Stage 1 in the music National Curriculum is:

> Pupils should be given opportunities to . . . make appropriate use of IT to record sounds. (DFE, 1995, p. 2)

Similarly at Key Stage 2 the only reference is:

> Pupils should be given opportunities to . . . make appropriate use of IT to record sounds. (*ibid.*)

Given the shortage of guidance from the National Curriculum in the use of music technology, it is important that teachers give careful consideration to the processes and content of the National Curriculum and consider ways in which music technology can support children's learning.

Explicit in the National Curriculum for Music is that children will learn through performing, composing, listening and appraising. There are key words to focus upon in No. 2 of the Programmes of Study for music in the National Curriculum which I have emphasized here:

> — at Key Stage 1 — '. . . taught to listen with concentration, exploring, *internalizing eg hearing in their heads* and *recognizing* the musical elements . . .' (*ibid.*)

> — at Key Stage 2 — '. . . taught to listen with attention to detail, and identify musical ideas, investigating, *internalizing, eg hearing in their heads*, and *distinguishing* the musical elements . . .' (*ibid.*, p. 4)

The terms 'recognizing' and 'distinguishing' were explained by the music Working Group for the National Curriculum as:

> We expect that pupils will *recognize* and respond to a musical stimulus before they can *identify* and give it a name. The ability to identify should lead on the ability to *distinguish* differences, for example between melodies in major, minor or pentatonic modes. (DES, 1990, p. 18, para. 4.7)

'*Hearing in their heads*' is the only example in the National Curriculum of the meaning of 'internalizing'. The Music Working Group for the National Curriculum described 'listen and internalize' as a process and gave examples of:

sing a song, but stay silent for a middle line or phrase; listen to each
other's and the teacher's choice of records. (*ibid.*, p. 50)

I believe that, like me, teachers do not find either of these references to
'internalizing' particularly helpful. I would prefer to consider 'internalizing'
with the broader definition as 'making meaning' of music. I would again refer
the reader to Glover and Ward (1993), Mills (1991) and Swanwick (1988 and
1994) as excellent sources to develop her/his understanding of making meaning from music. Implicit then in the use of 'recognizing' and 'distinguishing'
is that children will 'know' music by a process of 'internalization' which will
require them to make intuitive, cognitive and emotional responses. In doing
this children will need to work with music itself and with the elements of
music that contribute to 'the sum of the parts'. An important dimension in the
use of the music technology is to help children in 'internalizing': to help them
get an idea in their minds of what it will sound like.

Incorporating Music Technology

So, what can music technology offer music education? The fundamentals of
what music teachers are about remain the same with or without music technology. Music technology, however, can enhance the quality of work that
teachers and pupils undertake. One of those fundamentals in children's learning in music is identified in No. 2 of the Programmes of Study at each Key
Stage; where children are engaged with the musical elements of pitch, dura-
tion, dynamics, tempo, timbre and texture; and, of course, combining these
within structure, i.e. in the business of making music. Music technology can be
used to help children interact with each of these elements. Teachers need to
be clear in their own minds about the ways in which they will use music
technology to enhance children's musical development in relation to each of
these elements.

Having referred to the elements of music and the use of music technology
in enabling children's interaction with these elements, I would like to go on
to consider the importance of teachers being selective about the music technology that they use and the reasoning behind this selectivity. One of the
reasons for being selective in the use of music technology is to ensure that
quality in music education is developed. No matter how good you are yourself
as a 'technologist', the educational factor in the use of music technology is
another dimension and this needs to be given careful consideration by teachers. There is the danger that the 'technologist' wishes to incorporate music
technology and brings it in across a breadth of the music curriculum without
pausing to reflect and consider the effectiveness of its use. Music technology
is no different from any other tool for learning in that it can be used well and
it can be used badly.

Very careful consideration needs to be given to the use of music technology at Key Stage 1. We know the importance and value of children in their formative years using their singing voices, using acoustic instruments to learn about the elements of music and developing their fine and gross motor skills through making rhythmic patterns and physical responses to music. All of these are important in helping children to 'internalize' music and music technology can never replace them. Kemp outlines this way of 'knowing music' (Kemp, 1990) and goes on to suggest three forms of music technology that are in keeping with this principle; drum pads, microphones and wind controllers. I would go further, however, and suggest that kinaesthesia is one way of 'knowing music' and music technology can supplement kinaesthetic experiences. For example, if music technology is used by children to explore pitch and 'invent' tunes, this should be additional to undertaking similar activities which make use of glockenspiels and xylophones. Teachers at Key Stage 1 might usefully consider ways of using music technology as an 'accompaniment' to children's work/performance/playing on acoustic instruments, body percussion or voices. The music technology might help keep a steady pulse, provide a rhythmic backing or even convert children's rhythmic patterns into a more musical experience by providing a full harmonic accompaniment in a chosen 'musical style'.

Music Technology as a Tool for Learning: Keyboards and Rhythm Units

Learning tools need to be considered for their potential and they need to be evaluated in the light of planned practice. To begin this process we can investigate the potential of music technology in terms of what it is able to do. A useful starting point is the music keyboard. Most keyboards offer basic facilities including a rhythm unit which can produce set rhythmic patterns, maintain a steady pulse and operate at different tempi. One of things teachers would consider, indeed some teachers believe this to be a draw back of music technology, is that the technology 'does it for you', or does it for the child. How can children learn if the technology is doing it for them? Is learning in music not something to do with children actually doing it for themselves, having to work it out themselves? This is where teachers need to be clear in their own minds about the nature of the music encounters that children have in the classroom. Do children have to be able to maintain a steady pulse themselves before they work with one on a music keyboard? Could the keyboard not provide children with a steady pulse to enable them to participate in a musical encounter? Working with that pulse and exploring different tempi might be beneficial to children who have not yet learned to maintain a steady pulse themselves. Perhaps we can use music technology to take children further, move them on. Music technology should not be seen as offering 'tricks' for music-making but as a tool for acquiring musical knowledge. Rhythm units, in keyboards or in the form of drum machines, can be used to allow children to work with rhythm patterns based on 2s, 3s, 4s, 5s, etc.

Until more recent times, researchers had given little or no thought to children's ability to perceive harmony. This was probably in part due to the nature of music in the primary school. With the use of instruments such as guitar, autoharp and chime-bars over the last twenty to thirty years, children have been given first-hand experience of harmony. The National Curriculum for music makes specific reference to chords at Key Stage 2 and teachers of this age group are looking for ways to help children perceive, understand and control chords. There is little doubt that one of the best ways of helping to children to understand the concept of a chord is through the use of chime-bars where the chord is seen to be made up of a number of notes. However, one of the best ways of letting children create and control chord patterns and sequences is through the use of music technology. The 'single finger' facility on music keyboards is useful in helping children create and control chord sequences but is no good for helping children to grasp the basic concept of a chord. The three-finger chord functions (sometimes called 'auto-chord') on music keyboards only allow the chord to sound when three notes are pressed. Not only does this reinforce the concept of the chord, it allows children to find the notes on the keyboard which make up particular major and minor chords and also allows them to explore other chords, such as diminished chords. When combined with the 'automatic accompaniment' feature, which will offer a choice of musical 'styles', the child is still able to control chord patterns without having the technical facility to play the chords in the traditional sense. That technical facility might be developed, if appropriate, through the use of the three-finger function as a stepping-stone to free use of the keyboard.

'Voices' and Sampling

It is not uncommon to find up to 100 'voices' available on an inexpensive keyboard. This immediately increases the 'sound palette': the colours for children to incorporate in their musical compositions. They can too explore the timbral properties of these sounds. However, some teachers would argue against the use of electronic sounds on the grounds of the quality of these sounds: they might be considered of inferior quality to acoustic sounds. This is ultimately dependent upon two factors: the quality of the sound in the first place and the quality of the playback equipment. There may be nothing that can be done about the former, but the latter is not insurmountable. Whilst we should always endeavour to give children access to the best possible quality of sound reproduction equipment, there is value in children discriminating and making their own judgments on quality in sound.

There are problems in combining acoustic with electronic sounds, in terms of balance and matching sound quality. One of the best ways in which children can learn about this is by recording group pieces by means of a cassette recorder and a microphone. They could do this with acoustic instruments alone in the first place to find out about balancing different instruments. When combining music technology with acoustic instruments, the 'playback' or sound reproduction needs to be 'balanced' in the same way as any other instrument. Whilst children and adults may often be happy to accept the sound qualities as they stand, because the music technology is helping to give an idea of how some musical ideas are going to sound, there are times when the sound quality itself will be of the utmost importance.

With the use of a synthesizer it is possible to create new 'voices'. This is not usually easily accessible to most primary teachers as a basic understanding of sound synthesis is required. A much more accessible and valuable form of 'voice creation' is sampling. This involves 'capturing' a short sample of 'live' sound and then reproducing it. Sampling allows children to work with some of the fundamentals of sound and to explore timbre in a different way. It also has an advantage of being 'my' sound: a sound that the child has chosen or made which can then be manipulated in a musical context. The technology reproduces the sound in a way that is controlled by the child, taking away a level of embarrassment that might be felt by the child by creating a distance between the child and the sound in a performance sense, yet allowing the child to feel a sense of ownership of the sound. Some keyboards are sampling keyboards: they have a built-in microphone, and/or a socket for an external microphone, to enable short sounds to be sampled. Although sampling can be done on the computer with appropriate software, it is currently most accessible in the primary classroom through sampling keyboards.

Processors

Use of effects units, reverbs and delays in conjunction with a microphone are useful devices that allow children to explore properties of sound and create their own musical effects. They have the advantage of functioning effectively when used with the human voice as the primary sound source. Like the sampler, this makes the sound 'personal', i.e. owned by the child, and the technology provides a 'mask': the child can hide behind the technology but still has to initiate the sound him/herself.

Sequencers

Another feature readily available on many keyboards is a 'memory' function. This is a basic form of 'sequencer' which allows one to commit a musical sequence to memory. The sequence might be a melody, a chord pattern, a rhythm pattern or any combination of these depending upon the degree of sophistication of the keyboard. There can be great value in having the technology remember and replay musical events: it can 'hold' things while the child works alongside.

The sequencer is one of the most popular functions of a computer. It is when children are able to use sequencers to build up layer upon layer of elements of sound, and are able to switch 'on' or 'off' particular layers, that they can try out things and work towards organizing sound into simple forms. The idea of structure as well as the texture can be handled well by the sequencer: children can explore which sounds are put together; which rhythms; melody and accompaniment; parts that weave; blocks of sound; chords.

To use sequencer software on a computer it is necessary to have a MIDI interface for the computer and to connect this to a MIDI keyboard or other MIDI devices. MIDI (Musical Instrument Digital Interface) is an agreed industry standard between manufacturers allowing one MIDI device to be connected to another by a MIDI cable which enables digital information to be passed between them. Effectively, something played on a MIDI keyboard can be 'recorded' by the computer sequencer and played back on any MIDI device. In playback, the original 'voicing', tempo or pitch may be changed. In addition, the normal 'cut', 'copy' and 'paste' facilities are available on the computer so that the 'track' may be copied and edited by the child at the computer. Although this facility is only available through MIDI, it otherwise gives greater flexibility and control to children than the use of a cassette recorder to record their musical ideas.

It is interesting that Lawson *et al.* (1994) found that recording was one of the least common music activities in primary schools. Of course recording cannot take place without the use of music technology, whether it is with a sequencer or in the form of a cassette recorder with a microphone. The reasons why recording is underused in music teaching is open to speculation. An important aspect of children recording their work and playing it back, is that it increases their familiarity with their own and each other's music. This in turn can help them to develop their own musical memory and gain greater insights into musical features.

In addition to sequencing software, there are a variety of software packages to run on computers that allow children to explore different elements of music, sometimes in the form of music games. Through such packages children can develop aural skills, access a variety of forms of music notation (including traditional) and develop their musical memory.

CD-ROMs

Lawson *et al.* (1994) cited listening to music by different composers as the rarest event seen in their research:

> Conspicuous by its absence was classroom work devoted to listening and appraising. This is not altogether surprising. There had been considerable resistance throughout the music and music education professions to the heavy weight of musical history inserted into the

Programmes of Study late on in the consultation process by the National Curriculum Council. Teaching observed during this study appears to reinforce the idea that large amounts of audience-listening and sustained attention to the history of music are regarded as inappropriate for children in primary schools. (p. 12)

I believe that one of the problems primary teachers encounter in this area, is how they can present listening activities of this kind in a meaningful way. One of the most powerful developments in the use of computers in music education is the use of CD-ROMs in this area. These are CDs which contain audio tracks and computer data. They allow for interactive presentations which allow children to explore pieces of music whilst finding out musical and historical facts about the music. They can contain images, video clips, notation and quizzes to accompany the music being played and so encourage the child to listen. This author has developed some software which allows children to choose extracts from ordinary audio CDs and create their own commentaries to accompany them. The development in sound and image synchronization is a rapidly developing area and it will not be long before there are suitable software packages available for use in primary classrooms.

Conclusion

There are some things in music education which can only be done through the use of music technology. There are other things done better without the technology. The relationship between music technology and acoustic instruments is an important one and should not be ignored. Music education is not something that is only delivered through music technology, nor should it ever be. If children's understanding is to develop, it is music technology in partnership with acoustic instruments that will best facilitate this. If music technology is used to help children access particular aspects of music, then children need to develop their own understanding of what it is that the music technology is doing for them to enable them to move further forward in their own musical development.

So it is when teachers have this sort of understanding of what music technology can facilitate, that they can begin to make effective use of the technology. They need to be selective about which aspect of music technology they are going to incorporate first in their own music teaching. The selection may come down to what is available to them in their school. Having access to a particular keyboard for classroom use, the teacher might take this keyboard home and find out what it can do in relation to rhythm, chord patterns or memory. Then the teacher needs to consider how he/she is going to use this to best effect in the classroom. The teacher needs to know the technology him/herself to get the best out of it.

Music in primary schools is sometimes accused of being divorced from 'real' music. Although music technology is only used in some forms of music-making in the 'real world', children can easily make associations between music technology and 'popular' music at Key Stage 2 are in the period of 'pre-adolescence' when they are becoming more aware of the society that they live in without having the bonding with 'pop culture' that is more typical in adolescence. Music technology can draw children into music-making in schools, particularly at Key Stage 2 when 'hands-on' the technology is more important to them than replicating particular popular music styles.

We should not underestimate music technology's 'drawing powers': not that Key Stage 2 music-making should only be undertaken through music technology, but music technology should become an integral part of music education at Key Stage 2. Another word of caution here. Research by Coomber, Hargreaves and Colley (1993) identified that the use of music technology in the secondary school was often seen by boys and girls as a 'male preserve'. Their research also showed that:

> . . . familiarity and previous experience are clear predicators of confidence in computing . . . (p. 133)

It is vital that primary teachers do not reinforce the view that music technology is a 'male preserve'. Girls should be encouraged to use music technology in non-threatening situations and positive attitudes to music technology should be promoted by the teacher.

References

COOMBER, C., HARGREAVES, D.J. and COLLEY, A. (1993) 'Boys and technology in music education', *British Journal of Music Education*, **10**, 2.

DES (1990) *National Curriculum Music Working Group Interim Report*, London, DES.

DFE (1995) *Key Stages 1 and 2 of the National Curriculum*, London, HMSO.

GLOVER, J. and WARD, S. (1993) *Teaching Music in the Primary School*, London, Cassell.

KEMP, A. (1990) 'Kinaesthesia in music and its implications for developments in micro-technology', *British Journal of Music Education*, **7**, 3.

LAWSON, D., PLUMMERIDGE, C. and SWANWICK, K. (1994) 'Music and the National Curriculum in primary schools', *British Journal of Music Education*, **11**, 1.

MILLS, J. (1991) *Music in the Primary School*, Cambridge, Cambridge University Press.

SWANWICK, K. (1988) *Music, Mind and Education*, London, Routledge.

SWANWICK, K. (1994) *Musical Knowledge: Intuition, Analysis and Music Education*, London, Routledge.

10 Against the Odds: Drama After the National Curriculum

David Coslett

In this chapter I will consider some of the issues affecting the teaching of drama in the primary school since the introduction of the National Curriculum. I will argue that, despite what has been seen as the downgrading of drama's place within the curriculum, a number of developments have occurred or are occurring which may help drama establish itself within primary schools. I will suggest that, even if progress is patchy, there are signs that drama is emerging from a period of neglect and uncertainty and that now, with the recent reordering of the National Curriculum and a growing confidence amongst teachers in their own understanding of good practice, the time is right for drama to reassert its importance in primary education.

Shortly after the introduction of the National Curriculum, one teachers' professional drama association, in what appeared to be a gesture of extraordinary bravura, organized a conference entitled 'Every primary teacher a teacher of drama'. It could be argued, though, that such a conference may have been inspired more by hope than any sense of triumph at drama's scant inclusion within the core subject of English. Drama teachers may have been doing their best to put a brave face on the profound sense of disappointment they felt at the failure to identify drama as a subject in its own right or, perhaps a more realistic expectation, the failure to secure its place within a generic arts component of the National Curriculum. Defending and proclaiming drama's place in the core curriculum might have been a way of galvanizing its members to continue the struggle for a more widespread understanding of the place of drama as part of every child's educational entitlement. But beneath the pressures of curriculum reorganization is a set of unresolved issues and misunderstandings about the nature and purposes of drama teaching that continue to be a substantial impediment to the development of drama in the primary school and it is some of these that will be discussed in this chapter. They are issues that feature in much of the writing on educational drama in the eighties but, because that discussion, sometimes bitterly partisan in tone, was often confined to an internal 'expert' audience, it fell short of providing generalist classroom teachers with a clear enough foundation on which to build curriculum drama work.

Curriculum development hinges on conviction and understanding and is progressed through appropriate strategic development or training. In the years leading up to the introduction of the National Curriculum, drama had not done enough, it seems, to articulate its aims and principles in a manner that was sufficiently accessible or convincing to promote its widespread use within the classroom. The National Curriculum documentation for English (DES, 1988) itself displays, at Key Stages 1 and 2, the kind of confusion about drama that may have been in the minds of many teachers at the time. What is clear from the document and its attendant non-statutory guidance, is an instrumental view of drama teaching as a service-agent to promote particular curriculum objectives mainly in the area of English Attainment Target One, 'Speaking and Listening'. This view survives in the recently published version of the curriculum (DFE, 1995). The documents, even allowing for their necessary brevity, betray a lack of understanding of the nature of the drama experience, even in the area of language acquisition and development which appears to be the major reason for its inclusion in the curriculum at all. So, what exactly is drama's relationship to the development of language and on what basis should we be positive about the linking of the two?

There are many teachers who will say that, despite recent attempts to 'free up' the curriculum, if drama is to establish its place in primary schools to any significant extent in the coming years, it will be through its continuing identification with the National Curriculum. As things stand, this means chiefly in the way drama contributes to 'Speaking and Listening' in English (as well as the more vaguely implied contribution it can make to subjects such as history and geography through cross-curricular work). The problem with this argument for many drama practitioners is not in the linking of drama with English or the other National Curriculum subjects per se, but in the lack of regard it implies for the true nature of the drama experience which, in common with the other arts, has, at its core, an essential concern with the making and appraising of artistic form. Of course, as a verbal art, the use of language is central to the drama process. The way language is manipulated to enhance the symbolic significance of a dramatic event or episode is a key activity in drama. The language itself has the potential to acquire a symbolic dimension within the metaphorical world of the drama. It was not the intention of the English documentation to suggest anything of this complex relationship between drama and language, designed as it was to lay out, in a fairly rudimentary way, parameters for the teaching of English. However, what was surprising was that it appeared to perpetuate the tired notion that language is developed in drama simply by giving pupils 'opportunities to talk for a range of purposes', opportunities to practise skills of communication for different audiences. It failed to suggest anything of the important role drama can play in the development of language by providing contexts that engage the thinking and, indeed, the feelings of the participants. As such it ignores the research and writings of Cockcroft and Wilson (1978), Fleming (1982) and Byron (1986) and favoured instead the unproblematic view of drama and language which emphasized the development of skills, drama simply providing an arena where those skills can be deployed. Fleming, basing his work on the writings of Britton (1970) and

Donaldson (1978), argues succinctly that language in drama develops most fully when an imagined context 'matters' to the participants, when the issues faced and the outcomes which result draw on the child's own understanding and experience of the world. When thinking is 'embedded' in a context that is accessible and significant for the child, then the task of articulating that thinking becomes much less of an abstract enterprise. Neelands (1984) similarly writes about the importance of drawing on the 'vernacular' experience of children when constructing drama work. He makes the point that drama relies for its content not on the actual, real-life experiences of its participants, but that the teacher, in structuring drama, will look for points of contact between the real experiences of the children (acquired either first-hand or through some other source, for example, television, books) and the imagined context of the drama. In this way the 'story' may be new but the thinking involved will have important resonances with the child's actual experience. As Fleming (1982) states:

> The importance of drama is that it extends the sphere of reference outside the familiar events of the child's life, but the language and thinking which is employed is embedded in the sense that due attention is given to feeling intention and motivation . . . The central importance of language in drama is in its relation to thinking embedded in a feeling context which draws on the child's past experiences but projects him into new situations. (p. 16)

Fleming points out that drama's contribution to language development is much more profound than simply providing contexts for talk in order to extend the use of vocabulary. In drama, the effect of the language used can be felt or its impact seen by the participants and so pupils have an opportunity to understand the power and depth of its significance. The quality of the language used, whether complex or relatively straightforward, inevitably becomes a concern of the participants, for its appropriateness to the drama or otherwise will quickly become apparent to them. And this is the unique relationship drama has with language development. Whether drama provides pupils with experiences of a range of uses of language which might encourage speculation, negotiation, debating or explanation is not the major issue. All of these activities, in addition to their use in drama, will quite properly be provided elsewhere in the curriculum. But as the use of language is a central element of dramatic form, it becomes a special focus for the pupils and teacher working as artists in the creation of the drama experience. Far from having some extraneous concern with language development, the teacher working in drama is directly confronting the issue of how pupils understand the implications of their use of language and strive to find ways of using it more effectively and appropriately. Nor is this concern for effective language use confined to the 'moment' during which the drama is created. The language used in drama itself is available as a focus for discussion and consideration when pupils, usually with their teacher, reflect on their work. Neelands (1992) is cautious about the the English Statutory Orders' approach to the teaching of literacy, criticizing the:

> preference for splitting literacy back into the discrete components of speaking, listening, reading, writing, spelling, handwriting etc. (p. 36)

He argues for the integration of language activities and suggests that using drama sharpens the thematic or topic-based approach to learning which has received much criticism. For drama to be successful it has to allow for the child's perspective on events to be paramount, so that what is being taught actually 'matters' to the participants. He suggests that some thematic work may have failed to take this general lesson into account:

> A theme achieves breadth and balance when it provides for both affective and cognitive engagement and when the unity of the theme, *from the child's point of view*, is stressed rather than its remaining as a collection of loosely connected activities. (*ibid.*, p. 37)

By referring to a number of worked examples he usefully illustrates the relationship between language and the dramatic context. The 'pressure' of the drama, through the development of new role relationships within the fiction, poses particular language demands to which children respond. This goes far beyond the creation of dramatic contexts for the practising of 'talk skills' and is directly bound up with the essence of the drama experience:

> In simple terms, despite its immediacy and concreteness, drama sets out to make a thought-provoking *representation* of reality; it does not seek to duplicate or be a kind of 'virtual reality'. Dramatic contexts are in this sense no different from pictures, sculptures, films or poems. As with these other forms of art, we are drawn not just to the plot or content, but also to the form, to embedded meanings, to the metaphor. (*ibid.*, p. 26)

It is in this world of symbol and metaphor that meaning can be constructed through the manipulation of roles, events and situations. And it is within this context, too, that an emotional response to the drama is engendered, where participants can begin to 'care' about the evolving fiction, where feelings provide as much of a spur to expression as cognitive processes. The importance of acknowledging the part played by feeling in expression is, of course, not unique to drama (although the manner in which it does this — through role-taking — is). Holt (1995), in discussing aspects of generalist art teaching in the primary school, encourages teachers to base their art work on direct experience which has moved children. He explains that:

> ... experience that 'moves' children is anything that makes a signifi-
> cant emotional impression upon them, and which therefore provides
> an opportunity for them to make an expressive response through the
> use of materials. (p. 254)

It is important to remember here that the response to experience within the arts is mediated by the structure and discipline of the art-form itself which exercises an essential restraint on what is expressed. When working within art or drama the child is not engaged in an outpouring of uncontrolled emotion, even though the depth of feeling and commitment to the activity which the child is experiencing is significant.

In discussing the opportunities presented for drama by the renewed focus on speaking and listening within English, we have already moved into another important area where drama can seek to be a more established part of the primary curriculum. The importance of placing children's learning within con-texts they find meaningful and which encourage an 'active' response, has long been recognized as a major strength of primary school practice. The introduc-tion of the National Curriculum and the sometimes cumbersome burden of assessment may have dented, but not diminished, the determination of teach-ers to preserve this approach to teaching and learning in their perhaps now wider repertoire of teaching strategies. It would be difficult to imagine sus-tained work in, say, history, geography or science which did not attempt to contextualize learning, perhaps through the use of objects, artefacts, problem-solving tasks or some other means of promoting 'hands-on' activity. Recently, Davis and Pettit (1994) have argued for the importance of a 'contextualized' approach to the teaching of primary mathematics and even acknowledge, in a useful chapter with Peter Millward, the part that drama can play in develop-ing children's mathematical understanding.

One of the prime opportunities for contextualized learning, and one which will be familiar to early years teachers, occurs within children's play. The connection between play experiences and drama is so close, that it is surpris-ing teachers do not appear to be making the transition from play to drama within the classroom, particularly within Key Stage 1. The importance of play for pre-school children has long been recognized as a major contributor to the development of their learning. More recently, Hall and Abbot (1991) have attempted to reassert the importance of play within the formal school setting. Whatever particular branch of play theory one might subscribe to, there can be little doubt that through play, particularly the kinds of activity that Singer (1973) defines as imaginative or make-believe play, children are engaged in a process of acquiring understanding of their experiences. In both drama and play, children are operating in a hypothetical mode, where the imagined world of the make-believe is made present through their language and actions. Within the safety of this constructed domain, they may be confirming or practising what they already know or testing out new thinking or unfamiliar concepts and experiences and seeking to place them within their existing terms of reference. Piaget, of course, has usefully describes these two orientations as processes of 'assimilation' and 'accommodation'. Hodgkin (1985) although acknowledging the debt owed to Piaget, suggests that the 'practice' view of play may have contributed to a distortion of the more complex nature of the play experience. He suggests that not enough attention has been paid to the exploratory nature of the activity, where participants oscillate between the familiar and the unfamiliar, the reassuring and the exciting, between what could be boring and what might evoke a sense of danger.

The advent of the National Curriculum might have been thought by some to challenge the place of play within what appeared to be a heavily prescribed curriculum, and Tyler (1991) suggests that some teachers were fearful that the enhanced role of assessment might give rise to an increasing formality in teaching styles that might adversely affect opportunities for play. Yet Tyler argues that an examination of the content of the Attainment Targets and Programmes of Study across a range of subjects in the National Curriculum, far from threatening the place of play in the early years, actually confirms that much can be delivered through play-based activity. He also notes that as a result of research in the seventies and early eighties, there has been a shift towards a more structured provision of play opportunities because of a perceived lack of 'cognitive challenge' in much of the work that was observed. He asserts that teachers of young children are now more aware of the benefits that 'skilful intervention and more precise monitoring' bring to children's play experiences. And it is here that the teacher of young children can be confident about becoming part of children's play activities to offer focus and challenge to children's thinking and begin to make the transition from play to drama. This must not be seen as a kind of negative interference. The role of the teacher when joining in with the play activities of children is certainly to add structure, but a structure that does not usurp the children's position at the centre of the activity and threaten their ownership of the experience. The teacher or other adult will be working sensitively and skilfully, using her knowledge of the children, so that any appropriate implications of the play situation may be pursued. The play must remain the concern of the children. If it does not, then they will disengage from the activity or, at best, continue with it simply to 'please teacher'. Above all, this approach to play demands from the teacher the willingness and confidence to enter the play state with the children. Hodgkin (1985) identifies four roles a teacher herself must learn to be an effective practitioner and the first of these he describes as 'playing the fool':

> Even the most dignified teachers will not be highly regarded unless, sometimes, they are able to play; not merely to smile and laugh, but on special occasions actually to play the fool. (p. 87)

Whether one puts it precisely in these terms or not, the capacity of teachers to be able to operate within the world of children's make-believe, is a key factor in helping them make the transition from play to drama. This does not mean that every play activity that children engage in must be used by the teacher as an opportunity to intervene. However there is no doubt that the changing view of play provision within the school context provides an ideal opportunity for teachers to increase the amount of drama occurring within the primary classroom.

Finally, in making the case for drama's capacity to contribute to the development of language and for its efficacy as a powerful learning context which has much in common with make-believe play, there is the danger that drama will become disassociated from its natural place in schools which is within the arts curriculum. Over the past twenty years — even longer — there has been much discussion about the nature of the drama experience and much has been made of drama as a method of teaching or a means of enriching work in other subject areas. Hornbrook (1989) strongly challenged and criticized the 'drama as method' view and the tendency to see drama as a process of personal exploration and self-expression which, he maintains, was an overriding preoccupation of school drama work of the preceding decades. Such a view, he maintains, has its origins in liberal, progressive notions of education which, coupled with new understandings in developmental psychology, emphasized the centrality of the individual in the learning process and its primary goal, the development of personal understanding. For drama this led to a preoccupation with naturalistic modes of expression (the group improvization) where the context was usually the examination of a social issue and the purpose, the development of personal insight through empathizing with individuals in the dramatic situation. Despite his perhaps unfair representation of the work of some important drama practitioners, Hornbrook's analysis served to highlight the fact that drama, in common with the other arts, has an orientation which is intrinsically objective in character. Its purpose is to make something! Far from encouraging children to simply lose themselves in the imagined experience of improvized drama, both teachers and pupils need to understand that the drama itself, as real as any book or painting, is explicitly available for scrutiny and analysis and that such consideration materially affects the ongoing development of the drama. In effect, the process of making drama is impoverished without acknowledgment and reference to the resultant product. Indeed, working with a sense of product is part of the essence of the drama experience. Now there is an obvious tension here, especially for primary school drama, for, as Bolton (1984) points out, the product of drama is most easily recognizable as theatre. Theatre carries with it connotations of rehearsing, line-learning and presenting to an audience, all of which can inhibit and depress the vitality and depth of children's work. There are occasions, of course, when the structuring of theatrical experience is entirely appropriate for children in Key Stage 2 and Key Stage 1 and, perhaps because it is easier to define, this kind of drama activity receives due attention within the English Statutory Orders of the National Curriculum. But even in improvized classroom drama, where the action is unfolding at the moment of invention and there is no intention to present the work to an external audience, the objective orientation of drama, the product dimension, is crucially present. Bolton argues that, rather than distinguish different kinds of dramatic activity, it is more useful to focus on the mental 'disposition' of the participants. All drama activity requires its participants to engage in some kind of performative behaviour. In theatre, that behaviour has a descriptive orientation, its intention is to imitate and communicate to an audience the required event or narrative. In classroom drama or what he calls 'dramatic playing', the intention of the participants is simply 'to be' in the situation. There is a sense, even when they have an idea of the framework of the drama, that anything can happen as the events unfold. However, they are still involved in presenting or sharing this behaviour with other members of the group. The participants are still engaged in 'making' the drama, they are, in an important sense, managing and sustaining a piece of dramatic action which can be distinguished from other forms of social interaction. It is definable and tangible, even if its existence is momentary. This idea is of more than academic interest to the classroom teacher. Only when it is realized that drama, even the most apparently spontaneous, is something that is made, rather than something that just happens, can the understanding develop that it has shape and structure, and even rules which govern its creation. On a practical level, this means that the story, that which is made in the drama, is malleable in all sorts of ways. It can be stopped and started again; it can be remade if there is a reason to revisit a previous episode; it need not be chronological in the way events and incidents unfold; and, most crucially perhaps, it need not always explore and structure events through naturalistic conventions. This critical understanding, then, of the very nature of drama is the basis on which the teacher is able to develop and employ a range of teaching strategies to enhance the quality of work. Drama is a managed event, even though it draws its vitality from the intellectual and emotional involvement of its participants. It does not rely, for its success, on chance or luck or the extrovert expression of individual pupils — although, as in any other curriculum area, it benefits from the enthusiasm of the class. It is forged out of the manipulation of the elements of dramatic form and the application of appropriate structures and teaching strategies. Such a realization may not, of course, be new to the teacher who regularly works with drama. But for teachers who rarely or never use drama in their teaching, such understanding is fundamental to sustained, successful work; working in drama becomes much more than the implementing of a collection of short-term or one-off ideas gleaned from the latest in-service course. Even in the initial training of primary teachers, unless underlying principles such as these are addressed, then often students, who are, on the whole, willing to employ a range of approaches to their teaching, succeed in only the most superficial work in drama which, in time, they abandon to cope with the 'more pressing' demands of the National Curriculum. Yet if they understand that process and product are inextricably linked, separated out only for ease of analysis, and this is common to other arts activity, they go some way to being able to build their own ways of working in drama, ways which can develop as their teaching experiences grow. It may be argued that the reluctance to recognize the importance of product in drama (or perhaps more accurately, the equating of dramatic product simply with the performed play) contrasts with a traditional over-emphasis on product in the other arts areas. The National Curriculum may have helped steer teachers towards a more significant understanding of process here and there may even be, now, opportunities for teachers working in drama, art, music and dance to develop further a shared vocabulary when discussing the different arts disciplines.

This chapter has argued that, despite the presence of what appears to be a crowded primary curriculum, there are still opportunities for drama to become much more evident in schools. The highlighting of the Attainment Target 'Speaking and Listening' within the core subject of English provides an entry into the very heart of the curriculum if teachers are prepared to take it. An understanding of the way drama, through the use of symbol and metaphor, can develop rich contexts for talk can only serve to encourage its more widespread use. The reemergence of the importance of play and, particularly, the recognition of the case for greater structuring and adult intervention in children's play provision, present further opportunities for teachers to work in drama with their classes. Finally, an understanding that drama is a disciplined 'making' process over which teachers and children can exercise control, will help to counter the fear that drama is concerned with the spontaneous outpouring of expression and allow it to be more firmly identified with other arts subjects.

References

Bolton, G. (1984) *Drama as Education*, Harlow, Longman.
Britton, J. (1970) Language and Learning, London, Penguin.
Byron, K. (1986) *Drama in the English Classroom*, London, Methuen.
Davis, A. and Pettitt, D. (1994) *Developing Understanding in Primary Mathematics: Key Stages 1 and 2*. London, Falmer Press.
DES (1988) *English in the National Curriculum*, London, HMSO.
DFE (1995) *Key Stages 1 and 2 of the National Curriculum*, London, HMSO.
Donaldson, M. (1978) *Children's Minds*, Glasgow, Fontana.
Fleming, M. (1982) 'Language development and drama in a new comprehensive school in the North-East' in Wootton, M. (Ed) *New Directions in Drama Teaching*, London, Heinemann.
Hall, N. and Abbott, L. (Eds) (1991) *Play in the Primary Curriculum*, London, Hodder and Stoughton.
Hodgkin, R.A. (1985) *Playing and Exploring*, London, Methuen.
Holt, D. (1995) 'Art in primary education: Aspects of generalist art teaching', *Journal of Art and Design*, **14**, 3.
Hornbrook, D. (1989) *Education and Dramatic Art*, Oxford, Blackwell Education.

Neelands, J. (1992) *Learning Through Imagined Experience*, London, Hodder and Stoughton.

Singer, J. (1973) *The Child's World of Make Believe*, New York, Academic Press.

Tyler, S. (1991) 'Play in relation to the National Curriculum' in Hall, N. and Abbott, L. (Eds) (1991) *Play in the Primary Curriculum*, London, Hodder and Stoughton.

11 Dance Teaching in the Primary School: Voices from the Classroom

Janvrin Moore

Dance in the Primary National Curriculum

This chapter begins with a short review of the position of dance within contemporary primary education. This looks at the placement of dance in the National Curriculum, and examines the development and changes that have occurred within the dance documentation since the introduction of the National Curriculum. At this point, several studies which provide information on how schools and teachers are coping with the implementation of the National Curriculum are considered briefly. In the second section of the chapter, there is a selection of personal accounts of the teaching of dance taken from interviews with a number of practising primary school teachers. These provide some interesting perspectives on the teaching of dance, both before and after the introduction of the National Curriculum. The information provided by these 'voices from the classroom' is then discussed in the final section, which — whilst acknowledging the inevitable limitations of such a small-scale study — nevertheless attempts to draw some tentative conclusions about the current position of dance within the primary school and offer some thoughts for the future.

Dance, drama, music and art are all art forms, but within the National Curriculum only music and art stand as foundation subjects. Drama and dance are still recognized as art forms, but they are found within the National Curriculum subjects of English and physical education (PE). In the National Curriculum document *Physical Education for Ages 5 to 16* (August 1991), dance is quite clearly recognized as an art form and appears as a distinct area:

> ... of all the activities in physical education, only dance as an art form in its own right is characterised by the intention and ability to make symbolic statements to create meanings. This ... distinguishes dance from other physical activities, and shares characteristics with music, drama and art. These art forms are the basis for children's artistic education. (28, p. 64)

Dance has been part of primary education for a long time and it has been taught under a variety of titles such as: 'expressive arts', 'movement', 'dance' and 'physical education'. However, the placement of dance under the umbrella of physical education in the National Curriculum is not a new phenomenon, as Curl (1991) recognizes:

> Dance educators would be the first to admit that dance as an art form was fostered within physical education some three or four decades ago and under the various titles . . . it rapidly grew and developed. (p. 10)

The teaching of dance — as suggested in Curl's quote — is not new to the primary school teacher. A survey (in 1991) by the Arts Council on behalf of the PE Working Party confirmed that the teaching of dance was well established, and noted that, of all the primary schools surveyed, 77 per cent provided dance for both boys and girls at some stage during their time at school' (para. 5.20, p. 11).

Despite dance being a relatively well-established part of primary education, the National Curriculum has nevertheless required a change of practice in most schools. In Key Stages 1 and 2, dance is now one of the compulsory activity areas. This means that schools cannot just offer dance at some stage during the pupils' time at school, but are instead required to provide the activity in each year of Key Stages 1 and 2. In point of fact, primary schools are now, for the first time, responsible for delivering the total dance entitlement for pupils in schools. This is supported by Brinson (1992) who confirms that dance is now effectively optional at Key Stage 3.

The National Curriculum not only brought about a statutory entitlement for specific activities, but has also brought with it a clearly defined statutory Attainment Target and Programmes of Study. The latter has provided the primary teacher with a clear indication of the knowledge, skills and understanding that their pupils need to have by the end of each Key Stage. Additionally, a statutory content framework is now provided for dance and the other compulsory activities. The provision of such a dance programme for primary teachers was expected to raise issues and problems, and these have been well documented.

For example, the PE Working Group's Interim Report (1990) identified a range of issues which needed addressing in more detail before the submission of the final report. One of these issues was the particular needs of primary education. When the final report (August 1991) *PE for Ages 5–16* document was being produced, there was much debate as to how primary teachers would feel concerning dance. It was thought that many would feel largely unprepared to address these new responsibilities, and that a major training effort would therefore be required if the reforms were to succeed. The Arts Council survey (1991), which was commissioned to inform the National Curriculum Working Group for Physical Education, found that 26 per cent of the schools would require immediate in-service training were dance to be compulsory at Key Stages 1 and 2. This awareness was reflected in the final report which reported that dance would have resource implications:

Some teachers of dance undoubtedly feel uncertain how to develop content, and their work appears to lack progression. Given the evidence forthcoming from the DES survey, we acknowledge that some provision will have to be made for in-service training. (para. 5.23, p. 11)

The Group then provided some guidelines on the nature of in-service training:

Priorities for National Curriculum related in-service training are likely to be concerned with the delivery of the process model, helping teachers to become more aware of the components of planning, performing and evaluating, particularly in relation to dance. Teachers will also need guidance in the assessment of pupils' work. (para. 13.11, p. 52)

The five teachers' personal accounts that will be presented later in this chapter will help to indicate how much in-service work has taken place in schools or has been demanded by schools pre- or post-PE National Curriculum. It will be of interest to see the extent of provision of dance courses at a time when — because of spending cuts and associated policy decisions — advisory services are often either missing (Croall, 1993) or else are under threat.

The National Curriculum Working Group also highlighted the need for support to be provided within initial teacher training programmes:

There is no doubt that many primary teachers are currently ill equipped to teach physical education. This is partly due to there being no requirement for the number of hours training they may receive in physical education . . . Once the requirements for the National Curriculum physical education are in place there will be an even greater need to improve the existing quality of initial training at primary level. (p. 52)

The first statutory document, *Physical Education in the National Curriculum* was published in April 1992, and like the music and art documents, it had a very much more relaxed format when compared to the other foundation subjects. Curl (1991) puts forward a suggestion as to the reasons for this change in format:

Perhaps this is the penalty of being last in the queue, where the pressures experienced by the core foundation subjects have filtered through and led to severe modifications and amendments to the remaining subjects.

The document for physical education came into force for Key Stage 1 (year 1) and Key Stage 2 (year 3) in August 1992. This was shortly followed by the Dearing Report (1993) and recommendations. As a result, the final revised version of the National Curriculum for physical education in England and Wales was published in January 1995. It had taken four stages and four documents before implementation could begin, and as the last of the National Curriculum documents to be published it, 'came at the end of a bombardment of initiatives' (Shaughnessy and Price, 1995).

Since 1991 there have been several surveys completed on the implementation of the PE National Curriculum. The Central Council of Physical Recreation (CCPR) and the National Association of Headteachers (NAHT) mounted a survey in 1991 of 20,000 primary schools within the state sector, which revealed that 65 per cent of the schools felt unable to deliver the Physical Education National Curriculum. A survey by Bennett *et al.* (1992) revealed that 37 per cent of teachers in their sample felt competent about PE, while 63 per cent felt that they were in need of 'some help' to 'substantial in-service'. When these teachers were asked what they felt were their 'most important in-service priorities in the next year or so', only 15 per cent indicated PE as a high priority. The 1993/94 review of OFSTED inspection findings for physical education (1995) also brought to light some of the positive and negative aspects that had been associated with the implementation of the PE National Curriculum in primary schools. However:

> Only children in KS 1, years 3 and 4 of Key Stage 2 . . . were required
> to follow the National Curriculum in physical education in 1993/94.
> (p. 1)

The main findings and key issues from the OFSTED review suggested that standards of achievement in relation to pupils' capabilities were rather better at Key Stage 1 than at Key Stage 2, but that pupils were rarely found to be experiencing the full range of National Curriculum in PE at either stage; that many teachers at both key stages were failing to provide opportunities for pupils to plan and evaluate their own work and that of others; that although some primary subject coordinators were effectively supporting colleagues, the influence of many was limited. Finally, it was noted that the assessment and recording of pupils' progress was weak in both Key Stages.

As a result of this work, a number of key issues were identified for primary schools. The most significant of these were that: (i) steps needed to be taken to ensure a full and balanced implementation of the NC at Key Stages 1 and 2; (ii) more INSET was required, in order to give primary teachers the confidence to teach the full National Curriculum at Key Stages 1 and 2; (iii) coordinators needed more non-contact time to provide support for their colleagues; (iv) schools should work towards achieving a better match between schemes of work and lesson content, as curriculum documents currently were typically failing to influence the work across the Key Stages; and, finally, (v) the quality of assessment, recording and reporting needed to be improved at all Key Stages, and that teaching should be informed by the results of such assessment.

These findings all have shed some light on how primary schools are coping with the implementation of the PE National Curriculum. However, it must be recognized that most surveys have looked at physical education as a whole subject. There have been very few which have concentrated on the implementation of dance, which is the focus of this chapter. However, Harrison (1993) has considered this area:

> Teachers and schools will approach dance in the National Curriculum from many different perspectives. Some may already be reasonably confident and will only have to make minor adjustments to meet the new requirements. For others, the changes will be greater, especially for the generalist classroom teacher. (p. 5)

The following section will provide details on whether, and how, a small number of practising teachers approach the teaching of dance, and whether they have made adjustments to meet the National Curriculum dance requirements.

Voices from the Classroom

Geraldine Jones (1993) has highlighted the need for primary school teachers' perceptions to be examined, because it is only the primary teachers who have direct experience of the demands made by the National Curriculum on their time, their expertise and on their children. At present these demands are still largely an unknown factor, especially for dance. It is hoped that the five teachers considered here will provide some information on the precise difficulties being faced by such practitioners in meeting the demands of the National Curriculum legislation in the activity area of dance.

The experience, knowledge, skills and enthusiasm that individual teachers bring to their teaching of dance can also be examined. These qualities could perhaps provide some indications as to how a greater richness and quality of dance teaching might be extended to a larger cohort of schools.

The teachers were selected so that a range of schools and types of practice were represented. Some details have been changed in order to preserve their anonymity, but the accounts that follow remain true to each teacher's experience and practice. All teachers have been provided with pseudonyms which are appropriate to their gender.

Sarah

Sarah has been teaching for five years, and has been in her present school for four years. The school is located within a city centre area, and has approximately 430 pupils, ranging from reception to year 7. There are two classes for each year group, with an average class size of between thirty-two and thirty-five pupils. Sarah teaches a mixed year 1/year 2 group and the children are all aged 6 by the summer term. The class size varies throughout the year, starting with a class size of twenty rising to around thirty-four/thirty-five after Christmas. The pupils come from a variety of homes, housing association and private. Generally parental involvement and expectations are low. Facilities for physical education are limited. For indoor work, there is one space available, which is also the assembly hall. This room is tightly timetabled, because it is used by all fourteen classes. When asked about how she felt about teaching dance, Sarah replied:

> dance does not terrify me, and when I feel I know what I am doing I enjoy teaching it, but it is not something where I think, 'yes, I know what I'm doing and I know where I am going and I know what I have to do'. It is something that I have to really think about. I am not confident that I am covering everything that I should be covering.

Sarah does not find the planning of dance lessons overly time consuming, and she puts forward several reasons as to why. One of her reasons is because her dance lessons are planned and centred on topic themes that are being covered in the classroom. Sarah finds that a topic does not provide her with a visual picture of pupils doing dance but that it does give her:

> starting points, questions that I can ask, words that I can use, ideas for music that I can use. It helps me to think of lots of movement qualities that I might want them to explore.

Another advantage of topic work is that it allows stories and poems to be the stimuli for a unit of work in dance. Although Sarah states that 'I have never done an isolated dance session, it has always been related to topic work . . .' she does also recognize that:

> . . . some topics do lend themselves more to dance. For example, at the moment we are doing the sea and this really does lend itself and I feel confident, but I am not sure if I am covering all the National Curriculum aspects that I should be covering.

A second reason is that Sarah, who is a music specialist, approaches the teaching of dance in a similar way to her music composition lessons:

> I explore different movement qualities first without any music, just as I explore different sound qualities before I compose. I try to think of some kind of music that would help the pupils with the movement qualities.

She also sees a strong relationship between gymnastics and dance:

> If we are thinking about high and low in gymnastics, I might take that further in dance.

Sarah calls upon a range of resources in her planning and teaching of dance. For example, she has recently used the 'Lets Move' dance programmes. She has used two of these programmes 'The Blue Balloon' and 'The Greedy Zebra', which proved to be a valuable resource because they:

> . . . provide movement qualities and music. I think these are good for people who are worried about teaching dance because they provide a starting point, and show how ideas can be developed. I would not use the programmes in isolation because I think they are rather narrow and because the time allocated for the children to explore and create is limited.

Sarah's own experience of dance whilst training was limited, and this material has not been used during her teaching career. Dance in her course consisted of:

> . . . stylized movements which you would build up. Firstly you would do it on your own, then with a partner and then you might involve some objects. There was limited creativity. Music was very much out, and if music was used it was incidental.

This caused a dilemma for Sarah who, as a music specialist, felt that if dance and music were put together that they 'should be inseparable'. However, despite the strong link that she sees between dance and music she acknowledges that 'you do not always have to have music to dance'.

As to the purpose of dance, Sarah appears very clear, and sees this as twofold:

> . . . There are the expressive and creative qualities for their own sake to be experienced by nobody but the group. Or there is work towards a performance, where pupils get used to being dancers as performers.

In relation to the National Curriculum documentation, Sarah was trained with the 1992 document, and so had no experience pre-National Curriculum. She reveals that she is not aware of how the PE document has changed, and that she is awaiting details of this from the PE coordinator. The school system is for the subject coordinator to provide each class teacher with details of what they have to cover in each year group. Guidelines, programmes of study and units of work are in the process of being developed. However, there are still problems in this regard, and Sarah declares herself:

... very unsure of how to assess dance, and PE in general. I do not know to specifically look for, and it would be useful to have some sort of list where I could pull out one point each week and observe my pupils. The problem is assessing all thirty-five pupils as it would be very superficial. With my age group I find it difficult to observe because I have to be so actively involved in the session.

Accordingly, she would like to have more guidance on assessment, and feels that this is not provided in the National Curriculum documentation. She hopes that the PE coordinator will produce a policy which will provide her with some guidance, both on content to be covered and on assessment methods. Finally, Sarah is happy with dance being a compulsory activity area, and concludes by saying that:

This might sound awful but it tends to be older members of staff who feel awkward, but that stands for PE generally, not just for dance. I am in a generation of teachers who knew right from the start that they had to offer dance to their pupils.

Ann

Ann has been teaching at her school for fifteen years. It is a small, three-class village school, with three-and-a-half teachers and a class size of between twenty-five and twenty-seven. The pupils are from a predominately middle class area, and there are high academic expectations from the parents. Facilities for physical education have recently improved. Previously, the PE area was the playground, which meant that if it rained there was no PE. The school then began hiring the village hall, but as financial constraints got tighter, other plans had to be considered. The building of an extension was not possible as the school is a listed building. Accordingly, the main school, a high Victorian building, had a false ceiling put in to create a classroom upstairs and a small gymnasium/indoor space for physical education downstairs. This new addition means that there is now a small specialist area for physical education, complete with wall bars and ropes. Ann teaches 6–8-year-olds and has twenty-six pupils in her class. Both class size and age of pupils vary year to year because the pupils are equally divided between the three teachers.

Ann did not enjoy her dance experience whilst training to be a teacher. She found the 'leaves blowing in the wind', approach uninspiring and embarrassing. This is one reason why she has limited involvement in the teaching of dance. However, Ann does teach country dancing for the annual May Day celebrations. It is a tradition at the school to have maypole and country dancing at this time, which the parents come to watch. Ann volunteered to teach country dancing because:

I just happened to have a tape and book and thought the dance would add to the May Day celebrations. Initial planning did not take time. Having listened to the music first, I recalled some previously learned moves and then taught them to the children. Clapping and rhythm is an important part of the learning. The experience for the children is one of copying rather than being involved in creative/expressive work. I am happier teaching this type of dance.

Other than country dancing, dance is not a regular activity within her PE programme. Ann feels constrained by the the National Curriculum as a whole:

With the eleven areas of the National Curriculum to cover, if one gave everything equal time this would give PE less than 10 per cent. You have to give the weighting to maths, science and English, so this gives PE even less time. Within PE there are three areas of activity in Key Stages 1 and six areas in Key Stage 2. Dance therefore has little time on the timetable and is, I'm afraid way down on priorities.

The availability of facilities also play a role in Ann's priorities. The school offers swimming as they have free use of a local company's indoor swimming pool. As a result, swimming is put above dance, even though it is not a compulsory activity at Key Stage 1. Similarly, gymnastics is also given priority:

I feel I already give PE more time than I should, but I do not mind that, but I have a reluctance to go into the hall and do dance with them when they are desperate to use all this lovely new apparatus that we have there.

The demands arise from the need to plan carefully planning is seen as another constraint; As Ann makes clear:

Without having a dance background I couldn't just go into the hall and do a dance session without reading up, finding stimulating music for the children to work to, and planning specifically what I'm going to do. All that would take time which I honestly have not got.

Ann talked about the most recent National Curriculum Primary Compendium that had emerged as a result of the Dearing Review. She had found this much more accessible than the original ten individual subject documents, and had consequently spent time in the summer holidays reading it. Even so, her knowledge of the dance programmes of study is very limited, because a colleague teaches this activity area for her. However, she does have knowledge of the other areas within the PE curriculum. Despite being uninvolved in dance teaching, Ann retains a real interest and enthusiasm for dance. She attends an annual schools' dance day and views dance performances in a local theatre:

I really look forward to the dance day, it is really inspiring and I leave thinking 'I would really like to do that sort of thing with my children'. When I look how much time and effort has gone into it, it is something I just cannot do, there is just not the time.

When asked what she would do if the colleague offering dance was to leave, her reply was:

I'd do something about teaching dance.

John

John's school is a combined first and middle school, where the children range from 5 to 12 years. It is situated in an inner city area, and the pupils come from a variety of backgrounds: council housing, private housing, housing specifically designated for single parent families and for people who have financial difficulties. Parental involvement is very variable. John teaches within the 7–11 age range, but has also taught pupils from years 3, 4 and 6. He has been teaching for six years. There are two classes for each year group, and John is presently teaching one of the year 4 classes. He and the other year 4 teacher work as a team when planning the pupils' work. Class size does vary, but twenty-four/twenty-eight is an average size. The National Curriculum was introduced as John started teaching, and he has therefore not taught without it. The National Curriculum framework was established and some subject proposals were released during his one-year Postgraduate Certificate in Education course. John is a science specialist and the science document was in its last proposal stage at the completion of his course. John experienced the introduction and implementation of the National Curriculum. His memories of this period are associated with:

. . . trying to read through the documents when they arrived, and thinking 'I cannot do this'. I have to do it slowly. Next time I plan I have to refer to it because there is no point in sitting down and trying to learn it.

John found that constant changes in documentation did not aid the implementation of the National Curriculum. For example, he noted that 'the science documentation changed so much, six documents in six years.' And had clearly found this a challenging and confusing time in his professional life. The constant upgrading of the core meant that other subject documents were often only briefly read to ascertain general approaches, programmes of study and attainment targets:

. . . titles in the documents gave away the intentions of the approach. For example in music I read the titles, 'Performing', 'Listening' and

'Appraising' and this gave me messages about the way I was going to approach the teaching of music.

In some areas of the curriculum, this perhaps understandable economy of effort clearly reached extreme proportions. When asked about his early response to the PE documentation, John replied that it was probably fair to say that he 'had ignored it.' However, when asked specifically about his feelings on being required to teach dance, his response was emphatic:

> I like teaching dance. I never even dreamt that I would be involved or would teach dance before I did my postgraduate course. It was this course that switched me into dance. I went into school wanting to teach dance.

On the Postgraduate Certificate of Education course that he had undertaken, the dance teaching consisted of:

> . . . an approach that was the opposite to the 'be a leaf' approach. Dance was about expressing something but not in an 'arty, express yourself' way. For me the crucial thing was taking dance away from set moves and good technique. Dance became what you wanted it to do. You could put simple structure on it, like building a little piece and repeating it in different ways. Dance in this format meant you were developing skills and that anybody can dance.

This style of teaching dance and the specific materials experienced on the course was clearly useful. Indeed, John described it as 'all I used in my first teaching post'; however, in due course, he found that he had 'run out of material because I was relying so heavily on it. I wanted to develop other areas and to turn elsewhere.' Fortunately, a visit from a dance adviser gave John new ideas and another approach. This involved teaching his pupils dances he had made up, and allowed whole groups of children to do the same movements at the same time. He found that:

> Some of the pupils liked this approach because it alleviated the pressure for them to create and be constantly responsible for their performance. This approach also taught them new movements and allowed them to focus on body posture and movement skills.

John sees dance as an integral part of his curriculum, but has no idea if what he offers in dance is related to the dance programmes of study in the National Curriculum document. He is aware that dance is one of the statutory activity areas, and would use this documentation as 'a lever for doing things which other people might not see the value of'. On the purpose of dance John concludes:

Dance provides pupils with an opportunity to be creative. For some pupils it is an avenue for enjoyment because they love dancing. They should be given a chance to do that, even if other children do not like it. Dance provides an avenue for achievement which I experienced, and feel that this opportunity should be offered to my pupils. Dance is another medium for looking at other aspects of the curriculum. Dance can develop the self discipline which is associated with performing.

Jo

Jo teaches in a first school, which is situated near the edge of a city. The pupils range from rising 5 to 8 years, and the number on role by the summer term is between 550 to 600. There are five classes in each year group. The pupils are mainly drawn from modest, privately owned terraced houses which are close to the school. Some pupils are from other areas of the city, because their parents liked the school and chose it for their children. Parental involvement and support is generally high. Jo teaches a reception class, and the numbers within it vary throughout the year.

In September, for example, there are usually two reception groups, then another two groups come in January, with a fifth group joining in the summer term. Jo held the post of PE Coordinator for the last three years. However, she has recently been appointed as the Special Needs Coordinator for the school, and has consequently handed over the role of PE Coordinator to another member of staff. When Jo started teaching at this school, although there was a member of staff who was in charge of ordering PE equipment, there was nobody who was particularly interested in PE as a subject. With the introduction of the PE National Curriculum, she realized there was:

... a real need to have a PE coordinator, and because of my interest I volunteered for the role. I am not a PE specialist, but I am a sporty person and I really like dance. I was the only member of staff interested in nurturing this area.

However, despite this level of enthusiasm and commitment, Jo did not realize that being a PE coordinator would be such a huge undertaking:

There was a lot of change going on within the school because of a new headteacher. I was also new, and the school was very traditional in its approach to PE. There were definite set patterns for PE.

However, shortly after being appointed to the role, Jo attended a two-day, Key Stage 2, PE coordinators' course which:

... was quite advanced for me, as my work and experience was at Key Stage 1. However, I got lots of ideas which I could adapt and pass on to colleagues. Through practical sessions I gained insight into how to set up workshops and how to help my colleagues.

Jo enjoys teaching dance and sees dance as:

> an opportunity for pupils to express their feelings. Dance also develops their awareness of how to move, and it helps with their motor control. For reception pupils, movement comes naturally and they enjoy using movement as a response.

Unfortunately, however, this positive attitude to dance education was not really reflected elsewhere in the school. Contemplating the staff's attitude to the subject, Jo recalled that most of her colleagues:

> . . . were terrified about dance. When I came to the school, dance was 'music and movement' tapes which were religiously followed. No other form of dance existed. The teachers did select tapes to fit the theme they were doing, which was positive. When it was suggested that we needed to do dance in a different way there was immense worry. 'No, I cannot do it', was a common response.

However, staff attitudes towards dance did change, albeit little by little, and over a three-year period. In retrospect, Jo feels that this change in practice and attitude was a result of a combination of factors rather than one powerful one, and was largely brought about by the teachers themselves, who 'responded and changed in their own unique way'. Soon after attending the PE coordinators' course, Jo organized a practical workshop for all the staff, and took the opportunity to make use of some expertise from outside the school:

> I did cheat a bit and invited someone in to do this session, but I am glad I did. They enjoyed it, and for some it was a turning point. I also enjoyed being part of the staff and sharing the experience instead of leading the course.

Jo also sought to widen the amount of dance expertise available within the school by encouraging her colleagues to undertake INSET courses in this area of the curriculum. For example, she encouraged a member of staff from year 3 to go on a two-day dance course, with extremely positive results:

> She came back absolutely inspired, but she had a very difficult class and said 'I wish I could carry out the ideas with my class, but I cannot because they are not used to working in this way'. However, this teacher was able to share ideas with the staff and was enthusiastic about changing and implementing some dance. She mainly relied on

country dancing which has a defined structure, and was appropriate for her year group.

Developing her role as Subject Coordinator still further, Jo began to work with her colleagues within the school. Initially she worked with those in her year group, and describes her general approach to such activity in the following manner:

Firstly, I would prepare a dance lesson plan and musical tape for my class. Then I would try it out and if it was successful I shared it with other teachers in the year. For some teachers I gave them the lesson plan and music and talked them through it. With other teachers we put our classes together and we would take it in turns to lead a session. Some teachers just took off. One teacher's response to working as a team was 'I did not like PE until I came to this school'.

In the other year groups, at least one teacher felt confident and enthusiastic about teaching dance. They — like Jo — shared ideas with their colleagues.

The headteacher requested that a whole school curriculum plan (WSCP) should be drawn up. All subjects were included in this plan. It was the role of the coordinators to write up and present finalized plans for their subjects. In response to this, Jo established a PE working party with representatives from each year group. The group had regular meetings and detailed PE plans were drawn up for each year group. An important part of this planning was concerned with addressing the delivery of the dance element of the National Curriculum:

The dance plans were discussed and written with reference to the PE document. At each Key Stage it was ensured that programmes of study and key stage statements were covered. I then compiled the information, and a plan was forwarded for the WSCP. The dance section for each year group contained a list of objectives (which were seen as ongoing), followed by topics or movement themes for each term. The school plan not only brought the staff together . . . For some teachers it made them realize that dance was not isolated but linked to topics and material being covered in other subjects. Dance, for some, had become cross curricular, and they gained confidence and began to enjoy dance.

As well as working in the above roles, Jo spent a lot of time compiling music for certain themes and topics. This was welcomed by the teachers who had found music a stumbling point because of the time it takes to find and to copy suitable pieces.

At Jo's school, dance is performed in assembly and in the Christmas production, and this has helped raised its profile for pupils, parents and teachers.

Student teachers have also been influential in developing the school's approach to the subject. One result of their involvement in the school is that they have provided class teachers with new ideas and they have also put on their own dance productions as well.

Jo does feel that the ethos and teaching of dance has changed in the last three years. She believes that there are teachers on the staff who are still coming to grips with teaching dance. When asked whether dance would have changed without the introduction of the National Curriculum, her view is clear:

> No, I do not think dance would have changed. Dance was going on in this school prior to the National Curriculum so there is no change there. In some schools the National Curriculum documentation led to examination of a subject's rationale, content and practice. In this school it did make us think about what we were trying to do in dance. This and the WSCP (which was in response to the National Curriculum), has led to a change in how we approach and teach dance. However, the process of subject reflection and examination could have come about because of a HMI visit, a dance adviser, or because of a our new head teacher. It is difficult to say. However, I did use the *PE in the National Curriculum* document when planning topics and the whole school curriculum, so it definitely did influence change at that level.

Gail

The school where Gail teaches is a very large first school which is situated in the city centre. The pupils range from reception age to year 3. There are five classes per year group, with up to 150 pupils in each year. It has been the governors' policy to keep class size to a maximum of thirty pupils. There has recently been an extensive new building programme at the school during which time the hall has been out of action. Despite this constraint dance continues to be accommodated in the two school canteens. Every class in the school is timetabled to have one dance, one gymnastics and one games session each week. These three sessions were established three years ago on the advice of the school's PE Coordinator. The PE Coordinator had attended a local education authority course, which examined the PE document and highlighted the existence and importance of the three activity areas.

Gail teaches a year 1 class and has been teaching in this school for three years. She was a drama specialist at college, and she enjoyed the dance aspect of the drama course. Gail does not feel she is particularly good as a performer, but she:

> ... really enjoys teaching dance, because of the children's response. They are so creative and imaginative. They can also develop good control of their movements.

Gail is clear on the purpose of dance:

> Dance offers a lot. It offers the pupils an opportunity to be creative and to express their creativity in their own individual way. If the teaching is good, pupils will show variety. If confident, the pupils realize that they do not have to do the same movement as the pupil next to them. Dance also teaches self discipline, control and, by the end of Year One, cooperative skills. Dance is not academic so children who are not good at reading, writing etc., can feel that they are able to shine.

She feels that her own love of dance rubs off on her pupils, who enjoy working in this medium. However, Gail is aware that her enjoyment of dance is not shared by all other year 1 colleagues, who are clearly much less confident in this area and consequently much more likely to fall back upon commercially produced material:

> . . . some are very wary about teaching dance, and prefer to use 'music and movement' tapes rather than prepare their own lessons.

Gail does not condemn the use of resources such as the 'music and movement' tapes referred to above. Indeed, she herself uses them on occasions when they match the topic being covered, but tends to use other dance stimuli and resources as well.

> At the beginning of the term we used a tape, then we used a book *On My Way Home*, and now the topic is about 'ourselves' so we are thinking about different emotions and the stimulus for this is music. We have music that makes you feel happy and music that makes you feel sad.

Within the school, there is an emphasis away from music as being the sole resource for dance, because 'traditionally, most teachers who are wary of dance think they need music'. There has also been a deliberate policy to provide a variety of resources for dance, to help staff to realize that they do not have to use music:

> You can use a poem, or a book, or you can use percussion. You do not have to have anything, just focus in on words or movements.

Examples of this varied approach to dance is to be found in the school's planning. For example, a spring topic involves traditional tales and legends. Each week the pupils are read a tale or legend. Two or three of these tales are used as a theme for dance. For *Sleeping Beauty* a manufactured package is used. This includes a scheme of work and music. *The Pied Piper* is also done, and Gail produced the lesson notes and music for this tale, which are shared and used by her year group colleagues. 'Magnetism' is also used as a topic in this term and no music is used. The starting point for this dance occurs in the classroom and then attraction and rejection are used in dance. An LEA published scheme on magnetism is referred to. 'Growing', a further area, is left to individual teachers to design. A lot of staff have gained confidence in the teaching of dance because it is now an integral part of the whole school plan. Gail believes that the linking of dance to planning and topics:

> . . . has helped everyone, even those who were happy with dance, because it has given the subject some structure. Before the whole school plan was implemented, I suspect like my previous school, dance was on the timetable and you thought 'Oh, it is dance, what shall I do this week?'. Now with the whole school plan it seems much more coherent, and there is progression rather than duplication through the school. The planning has also led to dance being approached in a wide variety of ways. Teachers are beginning to appreciate that dance can be done without music and that you can use other resources and stimuli.

Nevertheless, despite all the guidance provided in the school, Gail feels that there are still some colleagues who have yet to develop enough confidence to operate autonomously as teachers of dance. She describes them as individuals 'who feel they need the whole lesson provided, because it tells you what to do, what to say to the children, and what music to use'. Nevertheless, Gail is sympathetic towards teachers who find getting appropriate material and music difficult and time consuming. She understands that, for some people:

> . . . if you want to use music it is hard. First you have to find what you want and then get it onto a tape without pauses and clicks. All this can take a long time. When I did the music for *The Pied Piper* it took me most of an evening for each week's work.

Typically, the actual planning of a class dance lesson does not now take Gail as much time as formerly, as she now feels that she can take most of her cues from the developing situation within a dance session. However, larger scale work does still require more of her:

> I almost know what I am going to do. I know that I am going to have some kind of introduction, and because I feel confident about dance, I do not have to plan much more because I respond to the pupils. However, when planning a single lesson for the whole year group it would take me forty minutes or so. If I had to provide music it would take me all evening.

When asked about her knowledge and understanding of the PE National Curriculum documentation, and more specifically the dance element of this, Gail revealed that she had a reasonably clear view of what had taken place in this respect. She felt that:

> The dance section of the National Curriculum has not changed greatly at Key Stage 1. Dance, even after Dearing, is very much the same . . .

Conclusions

These personal accounts inevitably show that each teacher is unique. Not surprisingly, the life events and school experiences of the individuals concerned have made their relationships with dance different from each other. It is clearly not possible to make any claims or generalizations based upon five accounts, but some common themes do emerge, and these justify some recognition and discussion.

Firstly, the attitudes of the selected teachers were similar to those in a survey by Ross (1994) who showed that such practitioners showed 'little sign of serious professional or personal discomfort' when it came to the teaching of dance (p. 35). In some respects, this seems to contradict the widespread recognition noted earlier in this chapter that the prescription of dance within National Curriculum PE would necessarily require the provision of substantial amounts of time, resources and retraining for a large number of generalist class teachers before they were to feel confident to deliver National Curriculum requirement with regard to dance. In this regard, there is perhaps a need to reconsider the needs of generalists who trained before the introduction of National Curriculum, because those teachers in the sample considered here who had trained while the reforms were being implemented appeared to be much more at ease and confident with the framework and demands of the order. They also seemed to be rather more philosophical about teaching dance, as a comment from one of them would seem to indicate: 'I am in a generation of teachers who knew right from the start that they had to offer dance to their pupils.'

Within the five, there was only one teacher who was not teaching dance, but she too, felt little personal discomfort, due to the fact that she thought that she did not have to teach dance. It would of course, be interesting to follow this teacher and see how she responds to the statutory requirement to teach dance to all pupils within each year group. This naivety as to which activities are statutory in the PE National Curriculum is also reflected in the 1993/94 OFSTED findings. Perhaps such a lack of awareness could also have skewed the findings of existing studies such as those by Mawer and Sleap (1987) and Jones (1992) which examine the implementation of the PE National Curriculum. The saying that 'ignorance is bliss' could well be appropriate in this regard.

Smith (1994) saw the impact of the National Curriculum as 'a wave of responses to each subject Order and revision as they rolled in' (p. 175). However, what these conversations with teachers appear to have revealed is that, at least in some schools, the Statutory Orders for dance have clearly been taken on board and have resulted in positive responses. Of course, it would be interesting to detect differences in schools that have undergone an OFSTED inspection and those that have not, but that is unfortunately beyond the scope of this account. However, it is certainly true that the two teachers in the sample who responded the most to the PE statutory documentation are also those whose schools have been inspected.

Bennett *et al.* (1992) examined teachers' perceived competence in meeting the requirements of the National Curriculum subjects. His findings showed that the length of time that a subject had been in the National Curriculum was closely related to a change in the teacher's personal responses to implementation. As in Bennett's study, the sample teachers' perceived competence to teaching dance was examined using the model provided by Hord *et al.* (1987). This has seven progressive stages of concern associated with innovation, going from level 0, where an individual has little concern about or involvement in the innovation, to level 6, where an individual explores the possibility of major changes and alternatives. The five teachers all expressed features of concern regarding their teaching of dance a specified in the PE document. For example, both Jo and Gail appeared to be functioning at levels 5 and 6 in Hord *et al.'s* model, whilst the others were very much associated with the initial characteristics seen in levels 0 and 1. A possible extension of the investigation reported here would be to examine the relationship between implementation time and personal responses to the teaching of dance, especially as Harrison (1993) suggests that:

> Most of us, teachers and children, need practical advice and some degree of success before we have the confidence and competence to allow ourselves and others total freedom in any art form.

As to the sample teachers' responses to the purpose of dance, these were broadly similar to those of the teachers interviewed in work by Jones (1992), who:

> . . . seemed to be using the interview to clarify their own thoughts on the subject, which made these reponses difficult to analyze. Content and concept were invariably intermingled in the teachers' replies. (p. 8)

On the whole, the teachers' replies were pupil centred and focused on the expressive, creative and communicative aspects of dance as an art form. As such, their responses mirrored the 1990 Physical Education Working Group Interim Report, perhaps indicating that there is now some emerging clarity as to the nature and purposes of dance as a subject.

Most of the teachers in the sample seemed unaware of the National Curriculum documentation on the dance Programmes of Study, other than two, one of whom was a PE coordinator. Once again, it seems that this response was close to that of the teachers in Jones' 1992 sample, who made their own decisions about what to teach, with personal preference being the governing factor. Other factors influencing the content of dance programmes and lessons were topics and available dance resources, rather than documentation. The use of topics to structure dance lessons was clearly recognized by the PE working party (DES, 1996, para. 2.14, p. 13), and several of the teachers had used topics to initiate dance lessons. However, one concern that arises here is that dance taught in this way is in danger of becoming merely an extension of other work being carried out in the classroom — more of a cross curricular theme — rather than a subject with its own distinctive structure and content (Slater, 1993). This, of course, is not to say that such theme and topic-based activities, if taught well — cannot focus effectively upon different modes of learning or interpretation. A view clearly shared by Lowden (1989):

> What matters most is the teacher who understands the learning experience as a whole and can select and interpret parts of that whole as a worthwhile and appropriate content and activity. (p. 36)

Certainly, the topic approach appears to have given some of the teachers confidence in their planning and delivery of dance, and this should be recognized and made use of. The planning of lessons using topics and the national documentation in conjunction with each other is clearly a promising way forward here. This was the approach used, both by the dance coordinator, and a teacher whose whole school plan had included dance. In both these cases, it had been the structure and content of the National Curriculum which had brought about a change. This perhaps reflects the view of Graham (1992) that one of the beneficial effects of the introduction of the National Curriculum is the bringing about of 'improvements in the planning and standards of the curriculum' (p. 10).

As the 1995 OFSTED findings show, assessment of dance was an area in which all the teachers within the sample identified they would like more help and information. In general, they were unsure of what to look for and how to record and report. Accordingly, Assessment, recording and reporting emerge as a priority area for subject coordinators and in-service agencies.

Another area of concern which was raised within the group was that of music. For all five teachers, there were problems associated with music selection, use and preparation time. This is perhaps an area which needs more consideration in the production of dance resource materials. Certainly, one of the teachers that was interviewed felt that more education as to the role of music in dance would be a major step forward in the teaching of dance.

The type of support for the teaching of dance received by the sample teachers was identified as school-based LEA support, LEA courses, curriculum coordinator, colleagues, students on teaching practice and dance resource materials. Perhaps predictably, the range and type of support was similar to that received by year 2 teachers with regard to assessment and SATS in the study by Bennett *et al.* (1992). This indicates that the support received by teachers is predominately provided by the same sources.

The 1990 Audit Commission Report on rationalizing primary school provision identifies the limited numbers of teachers in small schools as a major impediment to their successfully implementing the National Curriculum. However, Vulliamy and Webb (1995) suggest that teachers at Key Stage 2 generally feel confident in teaching PE, irrespective of school size. These findings were in general similar to Bennett's earlier surveys (1989–91) of primary teachers' perceived competence in, and concerns about, National Curriculum implementation. One teacher (Ann), who was from a small school, did initially claim to be confident about PE. However, when asked specifically about *dance*, she revealed that her confidence did not stretch that far, and that she did not regularly teach the subject. This perhaps raises the issue of whether a problem exists in that the teaching of dance can all too easily remain hidden when the label of physical education is used. Indeed, this perhaps one of the reasons why physical education has apparently fared so well in the various surveys noted above.

There are also dangers in comparing the small school teacher and the other four with these surveys in that it was not until 1992–93 that the last three subjects, art music and PE became statutory. Shortly after this date the implementation of the Dearing Review caused a delay and subsequent revision of documentation which meant that it was not until 1995 that PE became a curriculum priority by becoming mandatory for all year groups at Key Stages 1 and 2. Maybe the responses to Bennett and Vulliamy only revealed curriculum priorities held by teachers at that time. Certainly, the same thought appears to have occurred to others, and Campbell (1993) expresses a note of caution about the 'tentativeness of the available research evidence about the implementation of the Statutory Orders'.

This perhaps raises questions about this account. Because the interviews with the teachers were completed only one or two months after the emergence of the final *Physical Education in the National Curriculum* document in 1995. There may also be some danger associated with accounts examining the implementation of National Curriculum documents, because so often these do not appear to look sufficiently closely at practice. Certainly, there needs to be a continuing and more extensive examination of teachers and pupils, and of the conditions of classroom teaching and learning. However, what this study has shown is a variety of reponses to the dance section of the PE document, as well as some indication as to how far the implementation has proceeded within a small number of professional situations.

Of course, the need for primary teachers to implement the teaching of a subject which had previously been ignored or at best optional within the curriculum is by no means a new experience; for example, Smith (1994) discussing the manner in which primary school science teaching has been affected by National Curriculum policy notes that:

> The position of science in the primary curriculum was changed by the significant increase in the status given to the subject and by the need for planning which identifies specific learning targets. There is certainly more science taught in primary schools, more breadth and more emphasis on knowledge as well as investigation (HMI, 1992). The statutory curriculum has obviously led to an increase in the time devoted to science and attention to the content of teaching. In this sense primary science is evidently richer and so is the curriculum entitlement of primary pupils. (pp. 174–5)

It is still early days, but it would be nice to think that the teaching of dance within the primary school might perhaps benefit in the same way.

References

ARTS COUNCIL (1991) *Dance in Schools: Partnership in Practice*, London, Arts Council Publications.

AUDIT COMMISSION (1990) *Rationalising Primary School Provision*, London, HMSO.

BENNETT, S.N., WRAGG, E.C., CARRE, C.G. and CARTER, D.S.G. (1992) 'A longitudinal study of primary teachers' perceived competence in, and concerns about, National Curriculum implementation', *Research Papers in Education*, **7**, 1, March pp. 53–78.

BRINSON, P. (1992) 'Badly out of step', *TES*, 6, March p. 24.

CAMPBELL, R.J. (1993) 'The broad and balanced curriculum in primary schools: some limitations on reform', *The Curriculum Journal*, **4**, 2, pp. 215–29.

CCPR and NAHT (1992) *A Sporting Chance: A National Survey of Physical Education in Primary Schools*, CCPR, London Publication.

CROALL, J. (1993) 'Music and the arts' *TES*, 17 September, p. xii.

CURL, G. (1991) 'Dance in the National Curriculum? — Yes, minister!', *British Journal of Physical Education*, **22**, 4, pp. 9–13.

DES (1991a) *National Curriculum: Physical Education Working Group Interim Report*, London, HMSO.

DES (1991b) *Physical Education 5–16*, London, HMSO.

DES (1992) *Physical Education in the National Curriculum*, London, HMSO.

DFE (1995) *Physical Education in the National Curriculum*, London, HMSO.

GRAHAM, D. (1992) 'Beware hasty changes and achievements of the National Curriculum', *TES*, 3 January, p. 10.

HARRISON, K. (1993) *Let's Dance: The Place of Dance in the Primary School*, London, Hodder & Stoughton.

HORD, S.M., HULING-AUSTIN, L., HALL, G.E. and RUTHERFORD, W. (1987) *Taking Charge of Change*, Alexandria, VA, ASCD.

JONES, G. (1992) 'Teacher perceptions of the National Curriculum for physical education in the primary school. Part 1', *Bulletin of Physical Education*, **28**, 2, autumn, pp. 6–14.

Jones, G. (1993) 'Teacher perceptions of the National Curriculum for physical education in the primary school. Part 2', *Bulletin of Physical Education*, **29**, 1, spring, pp. 7–11.

Lowden, M. (1989) *Dancing to Learn: Dance as a Strategy in the Primary School Curriculum*, London, Falmer Press.

Mawer, M. and Sleap, M. (1987) *Physical Education within Primary Education* (a volume of essays compiled by the PEA Standing Study Group on Physical Education in Primary Schools), Hull, University of Hull.

NCC (1992) *Physical Education Non-Statutory Guidance*, Sheffield, NCC.

OFSTED (1995) *Physical Education: A Review of Inspection Findings 1993/94*, London, HMSO.

Ross, M. (1994) 'The arts in the National Curriculum', *British Journal of Curriculum & Assessment,* **5**, 1, August, pp. 31–6.

SCAA (1994) *Physical Education in the National Curriculum: Draft Proposals*, London, SCAA.

Shaughnessy, J. and Price, L. (1995) 'Physical education in primary schools, a whole new ball game', *Bulletin of Physical Education*, **31**, 1.

Slater, W. (1993) *Dance and Movement in the Primary School*, Plymouth, Northcote House.

Smith, R. (1994) 'Richer or poorer, better or worse? How has the development of primary science teaching been affected by National Curriculum policy?', *The Curriculum Journal*, **5**, 2, pp. 163–77.

Vulliamy, G. and Webb, R. (1995) 'The implementation of the National Curriculum in small primary schools', *Education Review*, **47**, 1, pp. 25–41.

Notes on Contributors

Chris Burns was a Primary Teacher before moving into higher education. At present she is a Senior Lecturer in the Rolle School of Education, and works mainly in the area of language and literacy.

Valerie Clark has worked as a teacher of Drama and English. Her doctoral research was concerned with the relationship between bereavement and the moral and spiritual development of young people.

David Coslett previously worked in primary schools as a specialist advisory teacher for Drama. He is currently Chair of Performance Arts in the University of Plymouth's Faculty of Arts and Education.

John Gulliver was formerly County Adviser for Primary English in Devon. He now teaches at the Rolle School of Education, where he is also undertaking research into aspects of formal assessment.

J. Mark Halstead is Reader in Moral Education in the Faculty of Arts and Education at the University of Plymouth and Director of the Centre for Research into Moral, Spiritual and Cultural Understanding and Education (RIMSCUE).

David Holt was a Primary Teacher before moving to Rolle as Senior Lecturer in Education. His doctoral research was concerned with investigating the nature of primary generalist teaching in art, and he has continued to develop his interest in this aspect of primary education.

Elizabeth Wilton Housego worked as a Primary Class Teacher, language coordinator and an advisory teacher for language before moving into higher education. She is interested in the significance of story as a cognitive resource and the use of picture books in schools.

Stephen Howarth was formerly a primary head teacher. He is now Principal Lecturer in Education, and has taught on a number of programmes concerned with the organization and management of primary schools. He is currently seconded to OFSTED.

Mim Hutchings previously worked in Avon as an advisory teacher for multicultural education. She is now Senior Lecturer in Language and Literacy, and has a particular interest in children's stories.

Will McBurnie spent the early part of his career teaching music in combined schools. He is currently PGCE Programmes Director at Rolle, and has a particular interest in the development and application of music technology.

Rod Mackenzie worked as a Teacher and Head Teacher in several primary schools in Oxfordshire before moving to Rolle, where he is Chair of Contextual Studies in Education. He maintains an interest in creative approaches to teaching and learning.

Janvrin Moore has taught in both primary and secondary schools, and now works at a number of UK and foreign universities as a freelance educational consultant. She specializes in Physical Education and Dance, and works principally in the areas of undergraduate professional studies and in-service education.

Index

Prolog++

The Power of Object-Oriented and Logic Programming

International Series in Logic Programming

Series Editor

Keith Clark, Imperial College of Science, Technology and Medicine

Associate Editors

Bob Kowalski, Imperial College of Science, Technology and Medicine
Jean-Louis Lassez, IBM, Yorktown Heights, USA

Editorial Board

K Furukawa (ICOT, Japan)
H Gallaire (Bull Systems, France)
J W Lloyd (Bristol University, UK)
J Minker (Maryland, USA)
J A Robinson (Syracuse University, NY, USA)
S-A Tärnlund (Uppsala University, Sweden)
M H van Emden (University of Waterloo, Canada)
D H D Warren (Bristol University, UK)

Other Titles in the Series

Parallel Logic Programming in PARLOG: The Language and its Implementation   Steve Gregory

Programming in PARLOG   Tom Conlon

Advanced Prolog: Techniques and Examples   Peter Ross

Logic Programming: Systematic Program Development   Yves Deville

Deductive Databases and Logic Programming   Subrata Kumar Das